D1145050

CELEBRITY BAKE BOOK

CELEBRITY BAKE BOOK

Published by Accent Press Ltd – 2012

Recipes © Individual contributors – 2012

Compilation © Linda Morris – 2012

ISBN 9781908766502

Printed and bound in the UK by Butler Tanner and Dennis, Frome and London

Illustrated by Sarah Ann Davies

Designed by Madamadari.com

FOREWORD

Baking has always been such a pleasure for me and I am so delighted to witness its constant revival in recent years. It is inspiring to see people rediscovering the joy of baking homemade cakes, biscuits and sweet delights. The possibilities are endless! Whether you are baking a simple cake for the family to enjoy or a whole array of delectables for an afternoon tea party, the end result will be just as satisfying. The process of baking itself can be incredibly rewarding and hopefully the recipes in this book will encourage others to take up the challenge. So many celebrities have donated delightful recipes for this important project and I think it is wonderful that such an enjoyable pastime can be used to support such a worthy cause.

I wish The Ben Kinsella Trust every success for the future and thank The Baking Belles Committee for putting together such a fantastic collection of recipes for us all to enjoy.

Warmest wishes,

MARY BERRY

Celebrity Bake Book is a collection of baking recipes and sweet delights from a variety of celebrities, celebrity chefs, politicians and royalty. All royalties from the sale of the book will go to The Ben Kinsella Trust.

Without the help and support of the following people this book would not have come to fruition and I would like to thank them most sincerely for all their help and guidance.

My "Baking Belles Committee" – Ingrid Salida for encouraging me, volunteering to be our chief Home Economist and helping me along the way; Anouska Plaut, Lindsay Shaerf and Elisa Margolin for coming onboard and having faith in me. Michael Salida for his legal advice and as our chief "Taster". My husband, Councillor Paul Morris OBE, for his encouragement and for dragging me away from my computer at some unearthly hour on many many mornings! Hazel Cushion and all at Accent Press Ltd for their encouragement, enthusiasm and generosity. Mary Berry for agreeing to contribute the Foreword. Luke Collings at The Cake and Bake Show; Farah Batchelor at Cake International; Harriet Luter at Country Living Fair; Chris Hughes at Taste Festivals. James Steen for his kind help. Andrew Bloch at Frank PR for his advice. Nick Thorogood, Heather Peacocke and their team at the food entertainment channel, Food Network UK for sponsoring the book and whose help and support has been invaluable. All those celebrities who so kindly gave their time and took part in the Promos to promote the book on Food Network UK and, last but not least, all the contributors who have generously shared their favourite recipes with us. Without their support there would be no book.

We thank you, too, for buying this book and we hope you enjoy using the recipes for many years to come, while supporting The Ben Kinsella Trust in its aims to reduce knife crime in this country. We hope that Ben would have been proud of its creation and its ultimate accomplishment to raise funds for such a worthy cause.

With my warmest wishes,

Linda Morris

~ CONTENTS ~

CONVERSION CHARTS

OVEN TEMPERATURES

Gas mark	C	F	Description
1	140°	275°	very cool
2	150°	300°	cool
3	160°/170°	325°	warm
4	180°	350°	moderate
5	190°	375°	fairly hot
6	200°	400°	fairly hot
7	220°	425°	hot
8	230°	450°	very hot

WEIGHTS

Ounces	Grams
1	25
2	50
3	75
4	110
5	150
6	175
7	200
8	225
9	250
10	275
11	315
12	350
13	365
14	400
15	425
16/1lb	450

VOLUMES

Fluid Ounces	Millilitres
1	24
2	55
3	75
4	120
5	150
6	175
7	200
8	225
9	250
10	275
15	425
20/1pint	570
1¼ pints	725
1½ pints	850
1¾ pints	1 litre

CAKES

TWIGGY
Model / Actress

Coconut Cake

My mum used to make a coconut cake on special occasions. The taste and smell of this cake takes me immediately back to my childhood and happy memories.

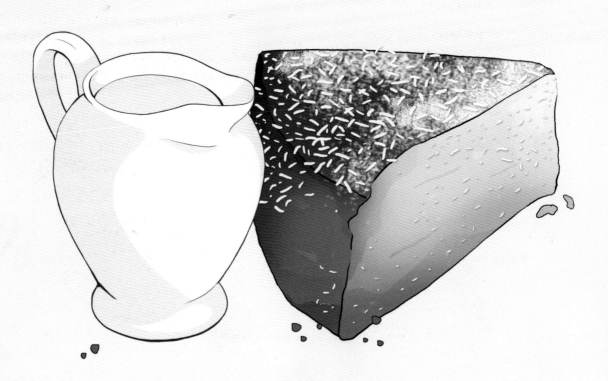

~ INGREDIENTS ~

- 200g plain flour
- 50g desiccated coconut
- ½ tsp salt
- 2 tsp baking powder
- 75g sugar
- 75g butter
- ½ tsp lemon zest
- 1 egg
- 125ml milk
- 1 tsp vanilla extract

~ METHOD ~

1. Pre-heat oven to 180°C/350°F/Gas 4.

2. Sift flour, salt and baking powder together in a bowl. Rub in butter until it feels like fine breadcrumbs. Add coconut, lemon zest and sugar.

3. In a separate bowl beat egg, add 100ml/3½ fl oz milk and vanilla extract.

4. Make a hole in the flour mixture and add liquid egg/milk mix. Blend altogether until mixture has a stiff consistency. Add the additional milk if needed.

5. Place in a greased 15x15cm (6x6in) cake tin and bake at 180°C/350°F/Gas 4 for 40 minutes or until an inserted knife in the middle comes out clean.

LORRAINE PASCALE

TV Chef/Author

Mini Tiramisu

INGREDIENTS

MAKES: 12

- 165g soft butter
- 100g light brown sugar
- 100g caster sugar
- 4 eggs
- 260g self-raising flour
- 80g ricotta cheese
- 3 tbsp coffee essence or 2 tbsp coffee dissolved in 4 tbsp water

- 12 amaretti biscuits, roughly crumbled
- Icing sugar and cocoa powder, for dusting

FILLING

- 500g mascarpone
- Seeds of 1 vanilla pod or 2 drops of vanilla extract
- 4 tbsp icing sugar

- 4 tbsp Marsala
- 8 amaretti biscuits, roughly crumbled

SUGAR SYRUP

- 165g granulated sugar
- 165ml /5½ fl oz water
- 2 tbsp coffee essence or 2 tbsp coffee powder

EQUIPMENT

- 12-hole muffin tin

'Baking Made Easy' by Lorraine Pascal (HarperCollins, £18.99)

METHOD

1. Preheat the oven to 180°C/350°F/ Gas 4. Line a muffin tin with 12 muffin cases.

2. Put the butter and sugars in a large bowl and cream together until light and fluffy. Add half the eggs, then tip in half the flour and stir well. Repeat with the rest of the egg then sift in the remaining flour. Add the ricotta, coffee and biscuits and mix well.

3. Using an ice-cream scoop or two dessertspoons, divide the mixture among the muffin cases. Spread the mixture flat with the back of a spoon. Bake in the oven for 25–30 minutes, or until a skewer inserted into the centre of the cupcake comes out clean. Remove from the oven and leave to cool.

4. The filling and syrup can be made while the cakes are baking. Mix together all the filling ingredients and set aside in the fridge. Put all the syrup ingredients in a pan over a low heat and let the sugar dissolve. Turn up the heat and boil for a couple of minutes or until thick, then remove the pan from the heat and leave to cool. Once the cakes are cooked, remove from the oven and leave to cool in the tin.

5. Once you can handle them, remove each cake from the case and slice in half horizontally. Put the halves cut-side up on a large plate. Brush each liberally with the sugar syrup. Go mad here, the cakes should be really, really moist. Keep the rest of the syrup to pour over the cakes at the table. Sandwich the halves back together with a generous dollop of the mascarpone cream, dust the tops with icing sugar and cocoa powder and serve straightaway.

WENDI PETERS
Actress

Cherry Bakewell Cake

This idea came to mind while on tour with Northern Broadsides Theatre Company. Every week I had been making a cake for 'Cake Club' and the actors could choose. We were chatting in the green room at the Salisbury Playhouse deciding next week's cake and one of the actors, Roy North (or Mr. Roy to us and many other Basil Brush fans of years ago), was chatting about Bakewell. I love anything with almonds in and added the marzipan for good measure!

INGREDIENTS

- 250g softened butter
- 250g golden caster sugar
- 4 eggs
- 150g self raising flour
- 100g ground almonds

- 1 tsp almond essence
- 100g glace cherries (chopped)
- 150g marzipan
- Raspberry jam (seedless)

FOR THE FILLING

- 125g soft butter
- 250g icing sugar
- 1 tsp almond essence
- Icing made up with water
- Glace cherries and flaked almonds to decorate

METHOD

1. Preheat the oven to 190°C/375°F/ Gas 5.

2. Grease two cake sandwich tins and line the base with baking parchment.

3. Cream together the butter and sugar until light and fluffy.

4. Add the eggs and beat well to combine.

5. Mix in the almond essence and then fold in the sieved flour.

6. Fold in the ground almonds.

7. Divide the mix between the tins and bake for 15 to 20 minutes until the centre of the sponge springs back on touch.

8. Allow to cool for 5 minutes then turn out onto a cooling rack.

TO MAKE THE BUTTERCREAM

1. Beat together 125g soft butter with 250g icing sugar and the almond essence until light and creamy (add a little milk if necessary). Put to one side.

2. Roll the marzipan into two cake-size circles about 3mm thick.

3. When the cakes are completely cool, slice through them.

4. Fix two sponges together with jam, one marzipan circle and almond buttercream. Spread more jam on top of this cake and then a thin layer of buttercream. Put another layer of cake on top and spread with jam, the remaining marzipan circle and then the buttercream. Put the remaining cake on top of that (there should be 4 layers of cake in total). Make up some icing with a little water to spread over the top and decorate with the flaked almonds and glace cherries.

Photo – Miki Duisterhof

DELIA SMITH CBE

Cookery Writer, TV Presenter

Banana and Walnut Loaf

I always think this is a good cake for eating out of doors, or taking on a picnic, as the bananas give it a very pronounced flavour.

~ INGREDIENTS ~

- 40g butter
- 40g lard
- 110g caster sugar
- 1 large egg, beaten
- Grated rind of 1 orange and 1 lemon
- 225g plain flour
- 2 level tsp baking powder
- 4 medium Fairtrade bananas, peeled
- 50g walnuts, roughly chopped

~ METHOD ~

Pre-heat the oven to 180°C/350°F/Gas Mark 4.

For this you'll need a 2lb loaf tin, base measurement 9.5cmx16cm, well buttered

Cream the butter and lard with the sugar till light and fluffy, then beat in the beaten egg a little at a time, and when that's in add the orange and lemon zest.

Sift the flour and baking powder, and carefully fold it into the creamed mixture using a metal spoon.

In a separate bowl, mash the bananas to a pulp with a large fork, then fold into the cake mixture together with the chopped walnuts.

Spoon the cake mixture into the prepared tin, level it off on top, and bake for approximately 50–55 minutes.

Leave the cake in the tin for 10 minutes then turn it out onto a wire cooling rack. Store in a tin.

© Delia Smith 2012 adapted from Delia Smith's Book of Cakes published by Hodder and Stoughton 1977 For further Delia recipes go to www.deliaonline.com

NIGELLA LAWSON

Food Writer/TV Chef

Birthday Custard Sponge

⁓INGREDIENTS⁓

UP TO 12 SLICES

- 200g plain flour
- 3 tbsp Bird's custard powder
- 2 tsp baking powder
- ½ tsp bicarbonate of soda
- 4 eggs
- 225g soft butter
- 200g caster sugar
- 2-3 tbsp milk

BUTTERCREAM FILLING

- 125g icing sugar
- 4 tsp Bird's custard powder
- 75g soft unsalted butter
- 1½ tsp boiling water

CHOCOLATE ICING

- 60ml water
- 2 tbsp golden syrup
- 125g caster sugar (or use 50g if using milk chocolate)
- 175g dark chocolate
- 1 pot hundreds and thousands

Birthday Custard Sponge recipe by Nigella Lawson, taken from "Feast: Food Which Celebrates Life", published by Chatto & Windus. Used by permission of The Random House Group Limited.

~ METHOD ~

1. Make sure everything you need is at room temperature before you start. Preheat the oven to 180°C /350°F/ Gas 4, and butter and line two 20cm/8in sandwich tins.

2. Put all of the above ingredients except the milk, into a food processor. Process to a smooth batter, and then add the milk a tbsp at a time to make a soft dropping consistency. Divide between the two cake tins and bake for 20 minutes. The cakes will have risen and feel spookily puffy; this is because of the cornflour in the custard powder.

3. Let the tins sit on a cooling rack for 5 minutes and then turn them out on to the rack, peeling away the paper.

4. **FOR THE BUTTERCREAM ICING**
Process the icing sugar and custard powder to get rid of any lumps, and then add the butter, processing again to make the buttercream come together. Feed the boiling water down the funnel with the motor running to make the filling easier to spread. Then sandwich the cooled sponges together with the custardy buttercream.

5. **FOR THE CHOCOLATE ICING** Combine the water, syrup and sugar

in a saucepan, stirring to dissolve over a low heat.

6. Let it come to the boil and then take it off the heat.

7. Break up the chocolate into small pieces if you are not using chocolate buttons (as I do for cooking, but good quality not confectionery standard), and then add to the pan, swirling it around to cover in the hot liquid. Leave to melt for a few minutes, and then whisk the icing to make it smooth and shiny. Pour over the buttercream filled cake, letting it drip down the sides, and then sprinkle generously with the hundreds and thousands before the icing sets.

8. Prong with candles, light them and sing.

LYNDA BELLINGHAM

Actress

Victoria Sponge

INGREDIENTS

- 225g butter
- 225g caster sugar
- 4 large eggs
- 225g self raising flour
- A few drops of vanilla essence
- A little milk, if needed
- For filling: strawberry jam, fresh whipped cream and strawberries

METHOD

1. Pre-heat the oven to 170°C/325°F/Gas 3.

2. Take two 7in sponge tins and line with silicone paper.

3. Using a wooden spoon or electric mixer, cream the butter and sugar until it is light and fluffy.

4. Add one beaten egg at a time to the mixture, beating well after each one is added.

5. Fold in the sieved flour a little at a time with a metal spoon.

6. Divide equally between the two tins.

7. Cook in the middle of the oven for about 25 minutes.

8. Cool on a wire cooling rack before spreading one layer with jam and adding the filling of cream and strawberries and sandwiching together.

9. Decorate the top with a few of the strawberries and cream.

10. Eat and enjoy.

HELEN LEDERER

Comedy Actress/Author

Chestnut Refridgerator Cake

INGREDIENTS

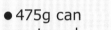

- 475g can sweetened chestnut puree

- 115g butter or margarine

- 28-30 sponge fingers (2 packets)

- 150ml strong hot coffee (made with 4 tsp instant coffee)

- 1 tbsp rum, brandy or Tia Maria

- 150ml whipped cream + 2 tsp caster sugar + 1 tbsp liqueur

- 125g plain chocolate

- Flaked almonds

METHOD

1. Put broken chocolate in basin over pan of hot water and leave to melt.

2. Cream butter and beat in melted chocolate.

3. Add sweetened chestnut puree.

4. Prepare 900g/2lb loaf tin (23x13x7.5cm/9x5x3in) or 20cm/8in round tin, 7.5cm/3in deep, by lightly greasing it and lining it with foil or greaseproof paper.

5. Add liqueur to coffee.

6. Divide sponge fingers into 3 groups and dip first group in and out of hot flavoured coffee and lay on the bottom of the tin.

7. Spread with half the chestnut cream and repeat with the 2nd group of biscuits and cream.

8. Lay remaining soaked biscuits on top.

9. Foil cover and chill until required. (Minimum 12 hours)

10. Run a knife around the tin to loosen the filling and turn cake onto chosen serving dish.

11. Cover with flavoured whipped cream and decorate with toasted flaked almonds.

OLIVER PEYTON

Restaurateur/Judge on the BBC's
Great British Menu

Raspberry Ripple Cheesecake

A deep red swirl of tart raspberry curd makes this cheesecake both delicious and striking. You could substitute almost any tart fruit for the raspberries. Rhubarb would work well, as would apricot or blackcurrant.

~ INGREDIENTS ~

BISCUIT BASE

- 250g digestive biscuits

- 90g unsalted butter

- Raspberry ripple:

- 200g fresh raspberries

- 80g unsalted butter

- 80g caster sugar

- 2 eggs

- Seeds from 1 vanilla pod

CHEESECAKE:

- 750g cream cheese

- 125g caster sugar

- 2 tsp lemon juice

- 100g soured cream

- 3 large eggs

SERVES 8 –10

PREPARATION TIME 20 MINUTES

COOKING TIME 50– 60 MINUTES

EQUIPMENT:

- 20cm springform/ loose-bottomed cake tin, about 7cm deep

METHOD

1. Preheat the oven to 170°C/Gas 3.

2. Crush the biscuits to a fine powder in a food processor (or put them into a plastic bag and bash with a rolling pin), then empty them into a bowl. Melt the 90g butter in a heavy-bottomed saucepan over a low heat, then pour it over the biscuit crumbs and stir to fully coat them with the butter.

3. Press the biscuit mixture into the base of the cake tin, then place in the fridge to firm up while you make the filling.

4. Purée the fresh raspberries in a blender or food processor and then strain them through a fine sieve suspended over a bowl, to remove the seeds. In a small, heavy-bottomed saucepan, melt the 80g butter. Remove from the heat and allow to cool for a minute. Whisk in the 80g caster sugar and then the eggs, one by one, mixing well after each addition. Add the vanilla seeds then stir in the strained raspberry purée and return to the heat. Whisk constantly until the curd thickens and just starts to bubble. Remove from the heat and pour into a shallow dish to cool. Set aside.

5. In a bowl, beat together the cream cheese, 125g caster sugar and the lemon juice until creamy. Mix in the soured cream and then beat in the 3 eggs until smooth. Remove the cake tin from the fridge and spoon half of the cream cheese filling mixture into it. Pour half of the raspberry curd in a layer over the cheese filling and then spoon the remaining cheese filling on top of this. Drop 4 separate tablespoonfuls of the remaining raspberry curd along the border of the cake and then a final spoonful in the middle. Insert a butter knife into the cake about 2.5cm deep. In one motion, zigzag the knife through the cake and the spoonfuls of raspberry curd to form a ripple pattern.

6. Bake the cheesecake for 50–60 minutes, or until the filling is set (it should be firm with just a slight wobble). Do not over-bake or the cake will split.

7. Remove the cheesecake from the oven to a wire rack. Run a small paring knife along the inside of the tin to release the cake. Allow the cake to cool completely before turning out onto a serving plate. Serve the cake at room temperature. Store any leftovers in the fridge for up to 4 days.

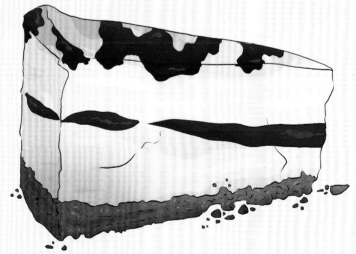

JANE ASHER

Actress/Author/Baker

Eccles Cakes

This recipe is a particular favourite of my husband's, and it works perfectly well with ready-made pastry – either fresh, frozen - or packet-mix if you don't want to make your own, as the sweet ingredients that it's filled with are quite enough of a distraction from any slight imperfections in the covering. In any case, most of the ready-made pastries and mixes are so good nowadays that I've pretty much stopped making my own for everyday pies and flans. (I never make the tricky and time-consuming flaky pastry any more: I feel about it rather as I do about calculators and long division - it's interesting and fun to do it a few times and understand the principle, but after that the quick way out is entirely justifiable...)

~ INGREDIENTS ~

MAKES

10-12 CAKES

- 40g butter
- 75g currants
- 50g mixed peel
- Pinch of nutmeg
- 450g flaky pastry
- Caster sugar for dusting

From her book, "Beautiful Baking", published by Simon & Schuster.

METHOD

1. Pre-heat the oven to 220°C/425°F/ Gas 7. Melt the butter in a small pan, or in the microwave, then add the fruit and nutmeg. Prepare a large baking tray by brushing the bottom and sides with a little vegetable oil and slipping a re-usable silicone liner (or a piece of baking parchment) of the right size in the bottom.

2. On a lightly-floured work surface or silicon sheet, roll out the pastry to about 1.5cm/¾ in and cut out large circles (about 10cm/4in diameter). Re-roll left over pastry as necessary until you've cut 8–10 circles.

3. Damp the edges of each pastry circle with water, and put a couple of teaspoons of the filling into the centre of each. Draw up the edges to the middle, enclosing the filling in little 'pouches'. Pinch the edges to seal, then trim away as much of the excess pastry as possible, or you'll end up with very thick bottoms to the cakes. Lightly flour the surface again and invert the cakes onto it, so that the joins are underneath. Roll out each cake very gently until they are flattened slightly and the currants just begin to show through the pastry.

4. Make two slashes in the tops with a sharp knife (or one… or three… opinion varies as to the traditionally correct number!), then brush with a little milk and sprinkle with caster sugar. Place on the baking tray.

5. Bake for 15–20 minutes until golden brown, then transfer to a rack to cool, sprinkling with a little extra sugar if desired.

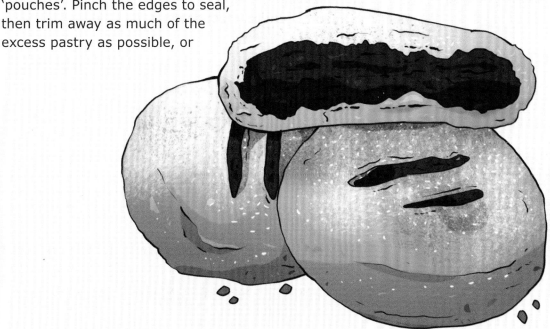

PAUL HOLLYWOOD

Master Baker/Judge on BBC's The Great British Bake Off

Blueberry Muffins

These are the best blueberry muffins ever. Leave the mix to rest for as long as your will power can bear...

~ METHOD ~

1. Cream the butter and sugar together then slowly add the eggs, mix for three minutes. Add the flour, baking powder, nutmeg, stir to combine, then refrigerate for at least an hour, preferably overnight.

2. Place a spoonful of muffin mixture into each muffin case, filling each to just over half way. Stud each muffin with about eight blueberries.

3. Bake in an oven set at 200°C/400°F/ Gas 6 for 20 minutes, or until golden on top. Serve with cream.

INGREDIENTS

MAKES 12

- 110g plain flour
- 110g butter
- 65g caster sugar
- 2 free-range eggs
- 1½ tsp baking powder
- 125g blueberries, or equivalent in frozen blueberries
- Pinch of nutmeg
- Double cream, to serve

DIANE ABBOTT MP

Shadow Minister for Public Health

Coconut Bread

INGREDIENTS

MAKES 2 X 450G/1LB LOAVES

- 115g margarine, melted, plus 1 tablespoon, for greasing
- 450g plain flour
- 1 tbsp baking powder
- 1 egg
- 300ml/10fl oz evaporated milk
- 175g caster sugar
- 2 tbsp caster sugar for glazing
- 225g desiccated coconut
- 1 tsp almond essence
- Pinch of salt
- 115g raisins (optional)

METHOD

1. Lightly grease two 450g/1lb loaf tins.

2. Heat the oven to 180°C/350°F/Gas 4.

3. Mix the flour, coconut, sugar, baking powder, salt, and raisins together in a bowl.

4. Beat the eggs then add to it melted margarine, evaporated milk and almond essence. Stir into the flour mixture to form a firm dough.

5. Divide the dough into the tins.

6. Mix the 2 tablespoons of sugar with 1 tablespoon of hot water and brush over the loaves.

7. Place in the centre of the oven for about 1 hour (checking that when a skewer is inserted it comes out clean).

8. Leave to cool. Then turn out, slice and serve.

Coconut bread is very sweet and dry; it can be served with butter as preferred.

ANJUM ANAND

TV Chef/Cookery Writer

Almond Cake

This is a lovely, soft and crumbly cake with the unmistakable hint of almonds. I discovered this recipe in a magazine over 10 years ago, adapted it to suit my tastes and it is now one of my favourites. It is rich so a little goes a long way and the nuts ensure that it remains moist for days in an airtight cake tin. Lovely with a cup of tea in the afternoon, but also delicious enough to serve guests with a little fresh or poached fruit and crème fraiche.

TV chef and cookery writer Anjum Anand has worked across the world in top class restaurants and has become a best selling author with her healthy take on Indian food. Last year Anjum launched her own range of Indian cooking sauces: The Spice Tailor.

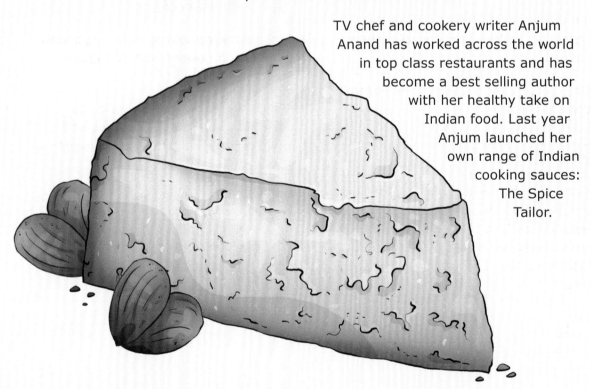

~ INGREDIENTS ~

- 150g plain marzipan, at room temperature

- 200g unsalted butter, at room temperature

- 140g caster sugar

- 3 large eggs

- ½ tsp vanilla essence

- ⅓ tsp baking powder

- 100g self-raising flour

- 200g almonds, blanched and peeled (or ground almonds)

- Pinch of salt

- Icing sugar to finish

- Crème fraiche (or other cream) to serve (optional)

~ METHOD ~

1. Pre-heat oven to 180°C/350°F/Gas 4.

2. Lightly butter and base-line with parchment paper, a round 20cm/8in cake tin.

3. Grind your almonds until they resemble crumbs.

4. Break down the marzipan in the food processor to soften.

5. Add the butter and sugar to processor and mix until creamy and then add the eggs in one at a time, mixing between each addition. You may need to add a tablespoon or so of flour towards the end.

6. Pour mixture into a large bowl and add the vanilla essence.

7. Fold in the remaining flour along with the baking powder, salt and ground almonds.

8. Pour into your prepared cake tin and place in the oven for around 60 minutes or until a toothpick inserted in the centre comes out clean.

9. Take out of the oven and leave to cool for 10–15 minutes.

10. Remove cake from tin and when cold dust with icing sugar and serve.

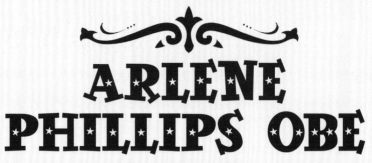

ARLENE PHILLIPS OBE

Choreographer

Gingerbread Cake with Mega Mix Icing

Follow me on Twitter @arlenephillips

INGREDIENTS

- 284g self raising flour
- 280g golden syrup
- 142g butter
- 3 tsp baking powder
- 1 egg & 2 egg yolks
- 200ml milk
- ½ tsp ground cloves
- 1 tsp ginger
- 1 tsp ginger extract

BUTTER ICING

- 90g unsalted butter
- 180g icing sugar
- 5g cocoa powder
- A little grated dark chocolate
- 1 tbsp coffee essence
- 1½ tbsp cranberry essence
- ½ tsp vanilla essence

TOPPING

- Bag mixed berries and nuts to scatter over top of cake.

METHOD

1. Pre-heat oven to 170°C/325°F/Gas 3 and grease three sandwich cake tins.

2. Put butter and golden syrup to warm in pan until dissolved. Stir, allow the mixture to cool.

3. Beat the egg and 2 yolks in large bowl with a whisk.

4. Add mixture to eggs and whisk together adding ginger extract.

5. Sift the flour, baking powder and spice into a bowl and add the milk, mix together well.

6. Divide the mixture into 3 buttered cake tins and bake in the oven for 16–18 minutes until cooked and the top springs back to the touch.

7. Leave to cool in the tins.

BUTTER ICING

1. Place the butter in a mixing bowl and beat or whisk until creamy.

2. Sift the icing sugar and slowly add into the butter beating well.

3. When the mixture is like a light cream, mix in the vanilla extract.

4. Split the icing mixture into 3

5. In one add cocoa powder and a little grated chocolate.

6. In the next, add a tablespoon of coffee essence.

7. In the third, add a tablespoon of cranberry essence.

8. Put the chocolate icing on the bottom layer, coffee on the middle layer and cranberry on the top.

9. Decorate with dried fruit and nuts.

JAMIE OLIVER

TV Chef/Food Writer/Restaurateur

Sticky Rhubarb and Ginger Cake

Photograph: David Loftus

You can get hold of rhubarb for most of the year – this forced stuff is so wonderfully pink and flavoursome that I just had to show it off on the top of this stunning cake. It's wonderful and moist, so it will keep well for a few days.

~ INGREDIENTS ~

SERVES: 10

- 200g butter, plus extra for greasing

- 400g rhubarb

- 100g caster sugar

- 2 tbsp stem ginger syrup

- 150g dark brown sugar

- 2 tbsp golden syrup

- 150ml/5fl oz/¼ pint full-fat milk

- 2 large eggs, preferably free-range or organic

- 300g self-raising flour

- 2 tsp ground ginger

- 4 tbsp stem ginger, finely chopped

- 2 tbsp of the rhubarb syrup

- Flour, for dusting

~ METHOD ~

1. Preheat your oven to 180°C/350°C/ Gas 4. Line the base of a 20cm/8in round cake tin with greaseproof paper, then butter and dust the sides with flour.

2. Slice the rhubarb into 4cm/1½in lengths and place in a pan with the caster sugar, 3 tbsp of water and the stem ginger syrup. Bring to the boil then poach over a low heat for 5 minutes until the rhubarb is soft but still holding its shape.

3. Meanwhile, melt the butter, brown sugar and golden syrup in a pan over a low heat. Once melted and combined, set aside to cool. Whisk the milk and eggs together then add the cooled butter mixture and stir in the flour and the ground and chopped ginger.

4. Pour the cake mix into the prepared tin. Carefully arrange the rhubarb on top of the mixture, reserving the remaining syrup for later. Bake in the middle of the oven for 1 hour and 20 minutes until risen and golden. If it looks as if it might catch, cover the top of the cake with tin foil for the last 15 minutes of cooking. To check it's cooked, insert a skewer into the centre of the cake – if it comes out clean, you'll know it's done.

5. Remove from the oven, spoon over the reserved rhubarb syrup and leave to cool completely in the tin before serving. Delicious with a dollop of crème fraîche or a helping of custard.

LOUISE JAMESON

Actress

Carrot Cake

~ INGREDIENTS ~

- 300ml/10fl oz honey
- 115g finely grated carrot
- 115g raisins
- 85g chopped dates
- 1 tsp cinnamon
- 1 tsp grated nutmeg
- ½ tsp ground cloves
- 115g butter

- 225ml/8fl oz water
- 225g whole-wheat pastry flour or fine ground whole-wheat flour
- Pinch of salt

- 2 tsp bicarbonate of soda
- 115g/4oz shelled walnuts, chopped
- (chopped almonds are an optional extra)

～ METHOD ～

1. Pre-heat oven to 180°C/350°F Gas 4.

2. Mix the honey, carrot, raisins, cloves, nutmeg, cinnamon, dates, butter and water together in a pan over a gentle heat, bring to boil and boil for 5 minutes. Remove from heat and leave mixture to cool for about 30 minutes or until lukewarm.

3. Stir flour and salt together in a large mixing bowl, then mix in the bicarbonate of soda after rubbing it in your palm to rid it of lumps. Add the chopped walnuts to the dry ingredients, make a well and pour in carrot mixture. Mix thoroughly until blended.

4. Pour into a well-buttered, lightly-floured deep cake tin, 23cm/9in square or 25cm /10in round. Bake in preheated oven, depending on the oven, this time can vary (especially with fan assisted) but I find 45–50 minutes seems to work. But do test if it feels firm at the centre when pressed lightly, and when a skewer is inserted and comes out clean (do test the centre of the cake).

5. Leave to cool for 10 minutes before turning out onto a rack - it is best eaten while still warm. You can top with a little thick cream whipped with honey and vanilla although I find this a little rich and prefer plain yoghurt.

LORRAINE KELLY OBE

TV Presenter

Dundee Cake

INGREDIENTS

- 300g plain flour
- 1 tsp cinnamon
- 1 tsp mixed spice
- ½ tsp salt
- 100g candied peel
- 100g cherries
- 480g currants
- 200g sultanas
- 200g raisins
- 100g blanched almonds (50g chopped: 50g whole)
- 4 eggs
- 4 tbsp milk or sherry or brandy
- 1 lemon, grated rind
- 200g margarine
- 1 tbsp black treacle
- 200g demerara sugar

METHOD

1. Pre-heat oven to 160°C/325°F/Gas 3.

2. Sieve together all the dry ingredients.

3. Mix the peel, fruit, cherries, chopped almonds and grated lemon rind.

4. Cream the margarine, sugar and black treacle until soft.

5. Whisk the eggs and milk (or sherry or brandy) together.

6. Add flour and egg mixtures alternately to the creamed sugar, margarine and treacle.

7. Stir in the fruit mixture.

8. Put into an 8–9 inch round tin, lined with double thickness greased greaseproof paper round the sides and at the bottom.

9. Tie a double band of brown paper round the outside of the tin, so that it stands well above the top of it.

10. Decorate with the whole almonds on the top of the cake.

11. Bake at 160°C/325°/Gas 3 for the first 1½ hours, then reduce to 150°C/300°F/Gas 2 for 1 hour or until a skewer inserted into the middle comes out clean. If not, return to the oven.

12. Leave the cake to cool in the tin and then turn it out, removing all the paper. Place on a rack to finish cooling. Wrap in new greaseproof paper and silver foil and store in a tin or airtight container. Can be eaten the next day but is better if left to mature for a few days.

RACHEL ALLEN

TV Chef/Food Writer

Irish Coffee Meringue Roulade

The word 'roulade' comes from the French word for 'to roll' (rouler). Roulades can be savoury – made with meat or vegetables and filled with various ingredients – or sweet: made as a cake or meringue and filled with fruit and cream. Meringue roulades make wonderful summer desserts. I love the combination of crunchy, chewy and creamy textures. The meringue can be made a day in advance and stored unfilled and covered with foil. Just fill and roll the roulade on the day you intend to serve it.

~ INGREDIENTS ~

SERVES 6-8

- 4 egg whites

- 225g caster sugar

- 50g desiccated coconut

- 1 tbsp instant coffee powder

FOR THE FILLING

- 425ml/15fl oz whipping cream

- 1 tsp instant coffee powder

- 1 tbsp sifted icing sugar

- 2 tbsp Irish whiskey

- 250–300g fresh or frozen raspberries

TO DECORATE

- Icing sugar, for dusting

- 23x33cm (9x13in) Swiss roll tin

Taken from "Bake" by Rachel Allen

~ METHOD ~

1. Pre-heat the oven to 180°C/350°F/Gas 4.

2. Line the Swiss roll tin with foil, folding the sides up to make a frame 4cm (1½ in) high and squeezing the corners together. Brush lightly with vegetable oil.

3. Place the egg whites in the spotlessly clean bowl (stainless steel is best) of an electric food mixer (or use a hand-held electric beater) and whisk until soft peaks form.

4. Fold in 1 tablespoon of instant coffee powder.

5. Add the sugar all in one go (but if using a hand-held beater, add the sugar in stages) and whisk at full speed for about 4–5 minutes until still peaks form.

6. Using a large metal spoon, fold in the coconut firmly and quickly.

7. Smooth the meringue into the prepared tin with a palette knife and bake in the oven for 15–20 minutes, until faintly browned and firm to the touch.

8. Allow the meringue to cool for a few minutes, then turn out onto a sheet of foil (slightly bigger than the roulade) – deftly turning it upside down onto the sheet and gently removing the foil on the base. Allow to cool completely.

9. For the filling; whip the cream in a bowl, fold in 1 teaspoon of instant coffee powder, 1 tablespoon of sifted icing sugar and 2 tablespoons of Irish whiskey.

10. Spread the mixture evenly over the meringue, leaving the long edge nearest to you free of cream about 4cm (1½ in).

11. Holding the foil closest to you, roll up the roulade away from you and leave it in the foil until you are ready to serve (it will hold neatly here for a couple of hours in the fridge).

12. When ready to serve, unwrap the roulade and gently push it onto a serving dish using a palette knife or cake slice.

13. Dust with icing sugar and serve.

MARCUS WAREING

TV Chef/Chef Patron,
The Berkeley, London

Pineapple Upside Down Cake

INGREDIENTS

FOR THE CAKE

- Pineapple rings
- 300g self-raising flour
- Pinch of salt
- 300g soft butter
- 300g caster sugar
- 5 eggs, lightly beaten
- Golden syrup

THE CARAMEL

- 100g caster sugar
- 20g glucose
- 20g water
- 50g whipping cream

~ METHOD ~

1. Line the base of a small round tin with a thin layer of golden syrup, place the pineapple rings on top, then put a ring mould or cutter around that, this will hold the cake mix on top while it cooks.

2. Cream the butter & sugar until light and fluffy then slowly incorporate the eggs.

3. Once smooth, add the flour and salt and mix well.

4. Spoon this cake mix on top of the pineapple, about 3cm thick and bake at 170°C for roughly 20 minutes. Keep checking them.

5. Turn out when ready and finish with some caramel.

6. Make the caramel with the sugar, glucose and water. Once dark caramel is achieved then slowly add the whipping cream, whisk until smooth.

JO BRAND

Comedienne/Writer/Actress

Banana Cake

INGREDIENTS

- 200g butter

- 340g caster sugar

- 390g self-raising flour

- 4 eggs

- 7 small bananas – mashed with a fork

- 1 tsp cream of tartar

- 1½ tsp vanilla essence

I particularly like this cake because you can just bung everything in the food processor and have almost instant results, apart from the tiresome 'cooking time' and 'cooling down time'.

I was intrigued too by 'cream of tartar' which the recipe demands – KC4H506 – an interesting culinary chemical with all sorts of healthy and worthy attributes which, I might assume, neutralizes the copious amount of vanilla ice cream or cream which lend themselves beautifully to the final baked cake.

METHOD

1. Put all the above ingredients in the bowl of the food processor with the beating attachment and whizz round for a couple of minutes until well mixed. Pour into a buttered or lined 8in/20cm or 9in/23cm square tin.

2. Cook for 30 minutes at 350°F/180°C/Gas 4.

ANNABEL KARMEL

Bestselling author on baby food
and nutrition

Goldfish Cupcakes

These chocolate cupcakes are delicious and
great to make with the kids.

Recipe taken from 'Annabel's Kitchen:
My First Cookbook' Ebury Press
www.annabelkarmel.com

INGREDIENTS

MAKES 10 CUPCAKES

- 125g butter at room temperature
- 125g golden caster sugar
- 110g self raising flour
- 2½ tbsp cocoa powder
- 2 eggs, lightly beaten
- 1 tsp grated orange zest
- 50g plain chocolate chips or plain chocolate chopped into small pieces
- 5 tbsp ready-made buttercream-style icing

FOR GOLDFISH:

- Cheerios
- Chocolate Buttons
- M&Ms (chocolate)
- Tube white chocolate writing icing or white writing icing
- Jelly beans
- Giant chocolate buttons
- White chocolate buttons
- Marshmallows
- Hundreds and thousands
- Heart shaped chocolates

METHOD

1. Pre-heat the oven to 180°C/350°F/Gas 4.

2. Beat together the butter and sugar until fluffy and smooth.

3. Sift together the flour and cocoa powder in a separate bowl.

4. Add the eggs to the creamed butter mixture a little at a time, adding a tablespoon of the flour mixture with the second egg.

5. Mix in the orange zest and the remaining flour and cocoa until blended. Finally, stir in the chocolate pieces.

6. Line a large muffin tray with 10 paper cases and fill each one until two-thirds full. Bake the muffins for 20–22 minutes. Allow to cool for a few minutes, then remove the muffins and place on a wire cooling rack. When cool, spread a little buttercream over each of the cupcakes and decorate to look like goldfish.

BARBARA WINDSOR

Actress

Sour Cream Topped Cheese Cake

~ INGREDIENTS ~

- 7in/18cm or 8in/20cm loose-bottom round cake tin or 8in/20cm loose-bottom square cake tin

- Small packet of digestive biscuits

- 25g butter

- 675g curd cheese

- 175g granulated sugar

- 3 medium eggs

- 1 tsp vanilla extract

- 3 small pots sour cream

- 85g caster sugar

～ METHOD ～

1. Grease the baking tin.

2. Crush the digestive biscuits in a plastic food bag.

3. Melt the butter.

4. Add the crushed biscuits to the butter and combine.

5. Place the crushed biscuit mixture into the bottom of the cake tin, and smooth over so that it is even.

6. Mix the curd cheese with the granulated sugar until well incorporated, add the eggs and vanilla essence and mix together (alternatively put the whole lot in a mixer and blend thoroughly).

7. Put the cheese mixture onto the biscuit base and bake in the oven for 25 minutes. The middle should be fairly firm, not too loose. If it is still loose leave it in the oven until the middle is not wobbly. (This all depends on the curd cheese. Some curd cheese is more loose than others, some are thicker and the looser the curd cheese the longer it will take to cook in the middle).

8. Take it out the oven and place it on a wire rack to cool for 10 minutes, whilst still leaving on the oven.

9. Mix the sour cream and caster sugar together and put carefully on top of the cake.

10. Turn off the oven and put the cake back in the oven for a further 10 minutes.

11. Take out the cake and leave to cool.

12. When cold put in the fridge in the tin. You can leave it in the tin until you are ready to serve. Decorate to your desired effect!

13. This cake is best made 1 or 2 days in advance. Chocolate digestive biscuits can also be used for the base.

CAKES 37

LINDA LUSARDI

Actress

Cherry and Almond Loaf

INGREDIENTS

- 150g butter, at room temperature, plus extra to grease

- 150g glacé cherries, washed, dried and quartered

- 125g natural coloured almond paste (or light-coloured marzipan), cut into 1cm cubes

- 150g self-raising flour

- 150g golden caster sugar

- 3 medium eggs, beaten

- 75g ground almonds

- Zest and juice of 1 small lemon

- 25g flaked almonds

METHOD

1. Preheat the oven to 180°C/160°C Fan/350°F/Gas 4. Grease a 900g loaf tin and line with baking paper.

2. Mix the cherries and almond paste with a tablespoon of flour to lightly coat. Set aside. Put the butter, caster sugar, eggs, ground almonds, remaining flour, lemon zest and juice in a large mixing bowl. Beat with a wooden spoon until just smooth. Fold in the cherries and almond paste.

3. Spoon into the loaf tin, level the surface and sprinkle with flaked almonds. Bake for 50 minutes in the oven, or until a skewer inserted into the centre comes out clean. Turn out to cool on a wire rack.

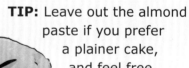

TIP: Leave out the almond paste if you prefer a plainer cake, and feel free to use undyed cherries or a mix of dried cranberries, blueberries and cherries.

ROSEMARY CONLEY CBE

Author/TV Presenter on
Exercise and Health

Blueberry and Lemon Muffins

~ METHOD ~

1. Preheat the oven to 150°C/300°F/Gas 2. Line a 6-hole muffin tray with muffin papers. Cream together the margarine and sugar in a large bowl using a whisk. Gradually mix in the egg.

2. Add the flour, baking powder and lemon zest, mixing with a wooden spoon and combining well. Mix in the skimmed milk and blueberries, then divide the mixture between the 6 muffin papers.

3. Bake in the centre of the oven for 20-25 minutes until well risen and golden brown. Mix together the lemon juice and sugar. Remove from the oven and drizzle with the lemon juice and sugar mixture.

INGREDIENTS

MAKES 6 MUFFINS

PREP TIME 10 MINS

COOK TIME 25 MINS

- 85g Lighter than Light Flora
- 85g caster sugar
- 2 eggs, beaten
- 130g plain flour
- 1 tsp baking powder
- 1 lemon, zest and juice
- 1 tbsp skimmed milk
- 100g fresh or frozen blueberries
- 1 tbsp demerara sugar

PER MUFFIN:
198 CALORIES
4.3% FAT

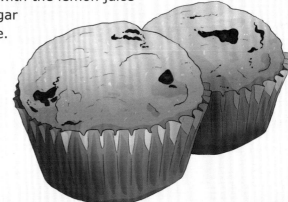

ADAM SIMMONDS

Head Chef at Danesfield House

Best Ever Lemon Cake

~ INGREDIENTS ~

FOR THE CAKE

- 310g caster sugar
- Zest & juice of 2 lemons
- 3 medium eggs
- 135ml double cream

- 250g plain flour
- 1 level tsp baking powder
- Pinch of salt
- 88g butter, melted

LEMON SYRUP

- 100g caster sugar
- Juice of 1 lemon
- 80ml water

LEMON GLAZE

- 125g icing sugar
- 2 lemons

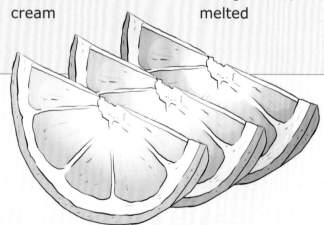

~ METHOD ~

1. Preheat the oven to 180°C/350°F/Gas 4.

2. Line a rectangular loaf tin (25x8cmx6cm) with greaseproof paper.

3. For the cake, mix together the lemon zest and the sugar and leave covered in the fridge overnight.

4. Add the eggs, double cream and the lemon juice to the sugar mix and whisk together.

5. Sieve together the flour, salt and baking powder.

6. Add to the egg mix and whisk, making sure there are no lumps.

7. Melt the butter and add to the cake batter.

8. Pour the cake batter into the lined tin and bake for approx. 40 minutes.

9. Check cake is cooked by carefully piercing the centre of the cake with a knife. When you remove the knife, the blade should be clean.

10. Place a cooling wire on a tray and turn the cake out of the baking tin.

11. Next, place the ingredients for the lemon syrup in a pan and bring to the boil.

12. Pour the lemon syrup over the cake (any syrup that drips down on to the tray can be poured back over the cake).

13. Then mix together the icing sugar, zest of 1 lemon and the juice of 2 lemons in a pan and warm very gently.

14. When the cake has cooled, brush over the lemon glaze and allow that to cool.

15. Return the lemon cake back to the oven for 5 minutes with the heat turned off to allow the glaze to set.

SIMON RIMMER

TV Chef/Restaurateur

Blueberry and Coffee Crumble Cake

❧ INGREDIENTS ❧

TOPPING

- 50g sugar
- 75g light brown sugar
- 1 tsp ground cinnamon
- 1 tsp powdered coffee
- 125g butter, cubed
- 225g flour

CAKE

- 150g butter
- 150g sugar
- 3 eggs
- 1 vanilla pod
- Zest of 1 lemon
- 150ml/5fl oz sour cream

- 250g flour
- 1 tsp baking powder
- 50ml strong espresso
- 1 tsp bicarbonate of soda
- 225g blueberries, tossed in a little flour

❧ METHOD ❧

TOPPING

1. Rub it all together.

CAKE

2. Cream the butter and sugar.

3. Add eggs, then add cream, coffee, zest.

4. Fold in flour, bicarbonate of soda and baking powder.

5. Spoon into a 225mm/8½ in cake or loaf tin, smooth the top, sprinkle the crumble on top. Bake at 180°C/350°F/Gas 4 for about 45minutes.

6. Serve with whipped cream or mascarpone.

THE RT HON THERESA MAY MP

Home Secretary and
Minister for Women and Equalities

INGREDIENTS

- 225g self-raising flour

- Pinch of salt

- 40g butter or margarine

- 25g caster sugar

- 150ml/5fl oz milk to bind

- 1 egg, beaten

Scones – Just As My Mother Used To Make Them!

METHOD

1. Pre-heat oven to 220°/425°F/Gas 7.

2. Rub fat into flour.

3. When mixture resembles breadcrumbs stir in sugar.

4. Bind with milk to a soft–not sticky dough.

5. Roll out and cut into preferred shape (I use a medium pastry cutter). Makes about 8–10.

6. Brush tops with beaten egg.

7. Place on greased baking sheet and cook in a very hot oven for around 8-10 minutes. You need to keep an eye on them as it is easy to overcook them and make them too dry and flat. They are ready when the tops begin to colour.

Baker/Patron of
Fancy Nancy Cake Boutique

Miniature Iced Gift Cakes

These pretty mini celebration cakes are really easy to make and are perfect for special dinner parties and presents to give away for Valentine's or Mother's day. Of course they make THE BEST homemade Christmas pressies too. They keep for months once iced!

This recipe will yield enough for an 8in square cake that will be able to be cut into approx. 14–16 circles for the centre. If you want to make a smaller amount, halve the recipe and make a 6in, but it's worth making a large fruit cake as it will keep for months and it's lovely to have with a cuppa! Or for a cheeky alternative, try serving the cake with some British cheeses and some dessert wine or port, the chutney quality of the fruit cake really compliments the sharp and savoury cheese.

This recipe is perfect for many occasions including birthdays and weddings but the beauty of this one is that it's so sticky and moist. You could of course cut out circles of any cake you wish, including my sponge recipe for cupcakes or a chocolate cake too.

Preparation time 30 mins. Baking time 3 hours at a low temperature.

Tip: Having all your ingredients at room temperature makes your cake recipe come together perfectly. If your ingredients are cold they will not combine well.

EQUIPMENT

- Weighing scales
- Large mixing bowl
- Wooden spoon
- Whisk
- Teaspoon
- Small sharp knife
- An 8in square cake tin (at least 22cm deep)
- Wire cooling rack
- Pastry brush
- Rolling pin
- Round cookie/pastry cutter around 2-2.5in diameter

INGREDIENTS

INGREDIENTS FOR AN 8IN SQUARE CAKE

- 240g soft unsalted butter
- 1250g molasses sugar
- 6 medium eggs, beaten lightly
- 1 tsp vanilla extract
- 800g raisins
- 550g currant or sultanas or mix
- 300g natural colour glace cherries
- 60g mixed peel
- Zest of 2 oranges
- 240ml good quality brandy
- 300g plain flour
- ½ tsp ground cinnamon
- ½ tsp ground nutmeg
- ½ tsp ground ginger
- ½ tsp mixed spice

ICED DECORATION

- 1kg marzipan
- 1 kg sugar paste in any colour you wish
- Icing sugar for rolling out
- Apricot jam (boiled in a pan on a hob or in a microwave)
- Brandy, vodka or cooled boiled water
- A sugar decoration (you can buy these ready-made in the supermarkets or you can make your own

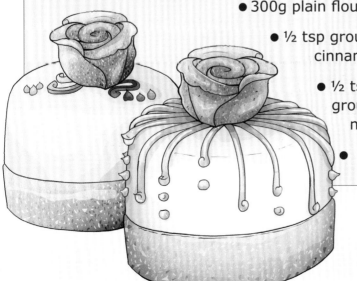

CAKES 45

～ METHOD ～

1. Wash the cherries and cut them in half.

2. Wash the fruit and drain through a sieve. Tip into a bowl, add the mixed peel and mix well. Pour the brandy over the mixture. Leave to steep overnight.

3. Preheat the oven to 140°C. Melt the butter and sugar together in a microwaveable bowl at 1 minute intervals, stirring each time until all the butter is melted and the sugar and butter have become amalgamated. Alternatively, do it in a saucepan, stirring until well mixed, then pour into a mixing bowl.

4. Add the eggs to the butter and sugar and mix again with a wooden spoon.

5. Tip the flour into a bowl and add all the ground spices. Sift the flour and spices mix into another bowl to combine them thoroughly. Now add the flour to the wet sugar, butter and egg mixture.

6. Tip in and stir the steeped fruit and remaining liquid, plus vanilla extract. Make sure you really mix well, use your hands if you find it easier to get stuck right in!

7. Spoon the mixture into the prepared tin and bake, 2½ –3 hours at 140°C/ Gas 1, until a skewer inserted into the middle of the cake comes out clean. Take notice of your cake while it's baking. If you feel it's getting very dark and cooked on the outside, turn the temperature down to 120 and bake for longer. All ovens vary greatly, so keep an eye on your precious cake! Leave the cake to cool in the tin, if you want to add an extra brandy kick, you can brush the top of the fruit cake with some extra brandy while it's warm. Turn out when cold.

8. TO STORE Wrap in a double layer of greaseproof paper and a layer of foil. This recipe is really rich and gorgeous, you don't have to leave it to mature if you are in a rush it will still be divine but of course a fruit cake improves with time so you can leave it to mature for 4-6 weeks if you wish.

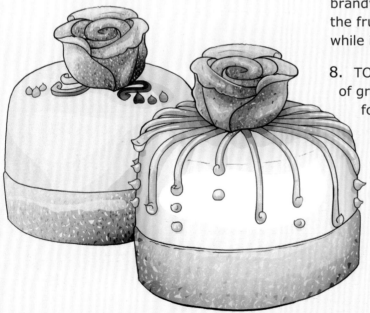

~ METHOD ~

TO DECORATE

1. Cut out little circular fruit cakes with your round cutter, they need to be about 2 inches high so if the cake is a bit deep trim down with a knife.

2. Brush the fruit cakes with some boiled apricot jam so they are sticky.

3. Halve your marzipan and knead on your worktop dusted with icing sugar and roll out to a thickness of approx 3-4 mm. Once you have rolled out you will have a large square. With a sharp knife, cut out smaller squares, big enough to lay over the top and sides of your mini cakes. Cut off the excess with a small sharp knife around the bottoms.

4. With 1kg you'll easily cover 12-16 cakes, if you want to make fewer just roll out less marzipan.

5. Place the squares on top and gently push down the sides to stick the marzipan, try not to pull down, but press onto the sides.

6. Pat the top flat and with the flat of your hands, work around the edges to smooth and straighten and give your cakes a good finish. If you want to try

for a more professional look, you can purchase cake smoothers, little flat paddles with a handle to make the surface really flat. You can buy these in many cookware shops now. Repeat the same process until you have as many as you need.

7. To ice the cakes, brush with a little brandy, vodka or cooled boiled water to make the marzipan sticky. Repeat the rolling out process with the sugar paste in the same way, cutting squares, placing over the cakes, trimming and smoothing until they are iced with a smooth surface.

8. Leave to dry overnight and decorate as required with a ready-made iced flower or decoration.

9. Any leftover fruit cake can be kept wrapped in baking parchment and foil for up to 6 months.

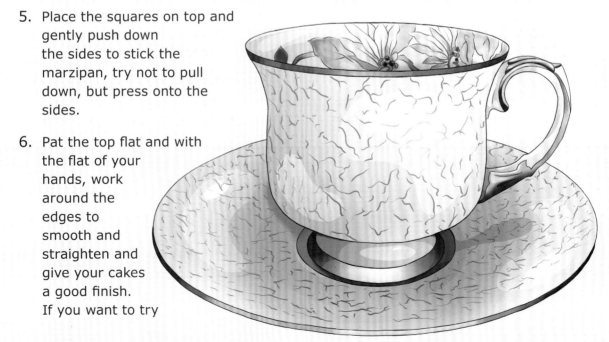

47

TAMZIN OUTHWAITE

Actress

Espresso Cake

- 240g caster sugar
- 240g unsalted butter
- 4 medium eggs
- 250g plain flour
- 1 tsp baking powder
- 600ml/20fl oz very strong coffee
- 150g caster sugar
- 60ml amaretto
- 250g mascarpone
- 100ml crème fraiche
- 1–2 tbsp icing sugar
- 40g toasted flaked almonds

METHOD

1. Pre-heat the oven to 160°C/325°F/Gas 3.

2. Grease and line a 22cm/8in cake tin.

3. Cream sugar and butter in a large bowl.

4. Slowly add lightly beaten eggs while gradually adding sieved flour and baking powder to prevent mixture from splitting.

5. Pour cake into tin and cook for 40–50 minutes.

6. Place a metal skewer through centre of cake and if it comes out clean, cake is ready.

7. Place warm coffee in a measuring jug and add sugar, stir until melted.

8. Add amaretto to coffee mixture.

9. When cake has cooled, prick all over with skewer and sprinkle over amaretto and coffee until the cake is almost saturated.

10. Leave cake in tin until all of the liquid has been absorbed.

11. In a glass bowl mix mascarpone with crème fraiche and icing sugar to taste and then spread over cake, sprinkling the toasted almonds on top.

Photograph: David
Griffen

JAMES AND CHRIS TANNER

TV Chefs/Restaurateurs

Gingernut and Mascarpone Cheesecake

Gingernut biscuits are not just for dunking in your tea! This quick cheesecake recipe tastes fantastic. Excellent served with chocolate sauce.

～ METHOD ～

1. Place the gingernut biscuits in a food processor and blitz to make fine breadcrumbs. Set aside. Line a baking sheet with cling-film.

2. Cut the vanilla pod in half lengthways and use the tip of a knife to scrape out the seeds into a mixing bowl. Add the mascarpone, caster sugar and cream to the bowl and whisk until smooth.

3. Place four 7x3.5cm deep metal chef's rings onto the lined baking sheet. Pipe or spoon the mixture into the rings and smooth off with a pallet knife. Cover with cling-film and chill in the fridge for 4 hours until set.

4. To serve, remove the cling-film from the top of the cheesecakes. Spread the biscuit crumbs onto a plate and dip the top and bottom of the cheesecakes into the gingernut crumbs. Heat the sides of the metal rings with a blowtorch or hot cloth and slide the rings off. Transfer the cheesecakes to serving plates and serve topped with a little grated dark chocolate or your choice of fruit purée.

JULIE ETCHINGHAM

Presenter, ITV News

Banana and Pecan Bread

~ METHOD ~

1. Heat oven to 180°C/350°F/Gas 4. Lightly oil 25x11cm (10x4in loaf tin).

2. Cream together butter and sugar until smooth. Add one egg and beat well, add the second and continue to beat well. Sift in half the flour with the bicarbonate of soda and salt, and mix well.

3. Mix in the milk, then the remaining flour.

4. Mash the bananas and then fold them into the mixture, and add in the vanilla and pecan nuts. Pour the mixture into the prepared loaf tin and level the top.

5. Bake for approx. an hour until a skewer inserted in the middle comes out clean. If the top of the loaf browns too quickly, cover it loosely with foil.

6. Allow to cool in the tin for around 20 minutes and then turn out. Beautiful and moist, the loaf can be served on its own or with butter – and will keep for days.

INGREDIENTS

- 125g butter
- 175g soft brown sugar
- 2 eggs
- 280g plain flour
- 1 tsp bicarbonate of soda
- Pinch of salt
- 125ml/4 fl oz milk
- 3 medium ripe bananas
- 1 tsp vanilla extract
- 75g pecan nuts, chopped

ANTHEA TURNER

TV Presenter

Easy Tray Bake

INGREDIENTS

- 4 eggs
- 250g soft margarine
- 250g caster sugar
- 350g self raising flour
- 4 tbsp milk
- 350g sultanas

If you're not a cake maker this is the recipe for you. My mum in the 60s used to make it when we were little and the little cakes disappeared nearly as fast as she could pull them out of the oven. It also appears in Mary Berry's Aga book but cooked in a baking tray which actually I prefer.

～ METHOD ～

1. Pre-heat oven to 180°C/350°F/Gas Mark 4.

2. Put all the ingredients except the sultanas into a bowl and beat for 2 minutes.

3. Fold in the sultanas and pour into a lined baking tray. I use a medium sized roasting tray, measuring approximately, 34cmx24cm (13½"x9½").

4. Pop in the oven and cook for about 20 – 25 minutes.

5. Take out when ready and let it cool before cutting into little square cakes.

6. Watch it disappear!

Recipe credit with courtesy of Mary Berry's 'Aga Cookbook'

INA GARTEN

Food Network Chef

Strawberry Country Cake

Photograph: Ben Fink

INGREDIENTS

MAKES TWO 8IN CAKES

- ¾ cup unsalted butter at room temperature
- 2 cups sugar
- 4 extra-large eggs at room temperature
- ¾ cup sour cream at room temperature
- ½ tsp grated lemon zest
- ½ tsp grated orange zest
- ½ tsp pure vanilla extract
- 2 cups plain flour
- ¼ cup cornflour
- ½ tsp kosher salt
- 1 tsp baking soda
- For the filling for each cake:
- 1 cup double cream (½ pint), chilled
- 3 tbsp sugar
- ½ tsp pure vanilla extract
- 1 pint fresh strawberries, hulled and sliced

METHOD

1. Preheat the oven to 180°C/350°F/Gas 4. Butter and flour two 8in cake pans.

2. Cream the butter and sugar on high speed until light and fluffy in the bowl of an electric mixer fitted with a paddle attachment. On medium speed, add the eggs, one at a time, then the sour cream, zests, and vanilla, scraping down the bowl as needed. Mix well. Sift together the flour, cornflour, salt, and baking soda. On low speed, slowly add the flour mixture to the butter mixture and combine just until smooth.

3. Pour the batter evenly into the pans, smooth the tops with a spatula, and bake in the centre of the oven for 40–45 minutes, until a toothpick comes out clean. Let them cool in the pans for 30 minutes, then remove to wire racks and let cool to room temperature.

4. To make the filling for one cake, whip the cream by hand or in a mixer until firm; add the sugar and vanilla. Slice one of the cakes in half with a long, sharp knife. Place the bottom slice of the cake on a serving platter, spread with half of the whipped cream, and scatter with sliced strawberries. Cover with the top slice of the cake and spread with the remaining cream. Decorate with strawberries.

SHAPPI KHORSANDI

Comedienne

Marble Cake
...my favourite
comfort cake

⤳ INGREDIENTS ⤳

- 225g unsalted butter
- 225g caster sugar
- 4 eggs
- 225g self-raising flour
- 3 tbsp milk
- 1 tsp vanilla extract
- (the expensive type makes a real taste difference)
- 2 tbsp cocoa powder

⤳ METHOD ⤳

1. Heat your oven to 180°/350°F/Gas 4.

1. Have a cup of tea. Grease cake tin (A bundt tin or one with a hole in the middle).

2. Mix butter and sugar together into a smooth paste. I don't care how nice it looks, DO NOT eat this.

3. Add the eggs and mix them in.

4. Sift flour into the bowl then the milk and vanilla extract. Mix it all up well. Divide the mixture into two separate bowls.

5. Add the cocoa in just one of the bowls and mix it up to make a nice chocolatey mixture.

6. Then, take a dollop of each and put them in the cake tin. Keep doing that so you've filled it with globs of chocolate and vanilla mixture. Take a chopstick or something similar and mix the mixture up into crazy swirls.

7. Put your head in the mixing bowls and lick clean. Pop cake tin into the oven for 45-55 minutes. If you put a skewer in the middle and it comes out clean, congratulations, it's done.

8. Let it cool nicely and have a big slice with another nice cup of tea.

REZA MAHAMMAD

Food Network UK Chef

Hazelnut and Raspberry Cake

~ INGREDIENTS ~

SERVES 8

- 50g plain flour

- 1 tsp baking powder

- 225g ground hazelnuts

- 3 eggs

- 200g caster sugar

- 200g unsalted butter, melted and cooled

- Juice and zest of 1

lemon

- 60g raspberries

- Icing sugar for dusting

~ METHOD ~

1. Into a mixing bowl, sift together the flour and baking powder, then fold in the ground hazelnuts.

2. Into a separate mixing bowl, whisk the eggs and sugar until very pale and fluffy, then gradually add the melted butter continuing to whisk until well combined.

3. Now fold in the flour and hazelnut mixture adding the zest and juice of the lemon.

4. In the meantime, butter a 23cm loose-bottomed cake tin, lining the bottom with baking paper, also greased. Pour the cake mixture into the tin and place into a pre-heated oven 160°C/325°F/Gas 3 and bake for 40 minutes.

5. Remove from the oven and allow to cool in the tin for 20–25 minutes, then turn out on to a wire rack to cool thoroughly. The cake should be slightly undercooked in the centre as the cooling process will help to finish it off.

6. Serve with either sour cream or crème fraîche.

EFFIE WOODS

Actress

Lemon and Almond Loaf Cake

INGREDIENTS

- 200g butter
- 180g caster sugar
- 3 eggs
- 100g ground almonds
- 75g self raising flour

- Zest and juice of two lemons

FOR THE GLAZE:

- 6 tbsp icing sugar

- 1–2 tbsp lemon juice

METHOD

1. Grease and line a loaf pan. Preheat oven to 180°C (160°C for fan ovens)/350°F/Gas 4.

2. Separate the eggs. Whip the whites to soft peaks. Using a mixer or electric hand whisk beat the butter and sugar together until fluffy and light in colour.

3. Stir in each egg yolk with a third of the flour - this helps to prevent the mixture curdling – until well combined, but don't over-mix.

4. Stir in the ground almonds and lemon zest (not the juice) and again, don't over-mix.

5. Gently fold in the egg whites, trying to keep as much air in as possible.

6. Spoon the batter into the lined pan and bake for 45–50 minutes - test with a skewer and if it comes out clean, it's done.

7. Now you have two options...

8. With a chopstick, pierce the cake in 10 or so places, then squeeze the juice of the two lemons all over it (leaving a little juice for the glaze). Leave the cake to cool in the tin.

THE GLAZE:

1. Mix the icing sugar and juice into a thin icing. Pour all over the cooled cake and leave to set.

2. OR Gently heat the juice of the two lemons with 4 tbsp of sugar until dissolved into a syrup. As soon as the cake comes out of the oven, pierce the cake in 10 or so places with a chopstick and pour the syrup over the top.

3. Either way, it's brilliant. If you use the syrup method, the cake will be über-moist, closer to a pudding. Wonderful if served with some whipped cream or Greek yoghurt. Store in an airtight container. This cake has the texture of a pound cake – it's very moist but still light. Because of the almonds this cake actually gets moister over time, so it's better on day two...

TONY TOBIN

TV Chef/Chef Patron,
The Dining Room, Reigate

Mum's Coffee and Walnut Cake

I have fond memories of eating this delicious coffee cake as a child. Easy to make and really hard to eat only one piece!

INGREDIENTS

- 225g butter

- 225g brown sugar

- 4 eggs

- 225g self-raising flour

- 50g walnuts, chopped

- 2 tbsp strong coffee (or essence)

FOR THE FILLING AND TOPPING:

- 65g caster sugar

- 4 tsp water

- 2 egg yolks

- 165g butter

- 12 walnut halves

- 1 tbsp strong coffee (or essence)

METHOD

1. Preheat the oven to 170°C/325°F/Gas 3.

2. First make the cake. In a mixing bowl, cream the butter and sugar together until smooth, light and fluffy.

3. Add a little flour and then mix in the eggs, one at a time, mixing thoroughly.

4. Slowly fold in the remaining flour, and then the chopped walnuts and coffee.

5. Divide the mixture evenly between two greased, base-lined 20cm sandwich cake tins.

6. Bake in the oven for 30 minutes until risen and set. Remove from the oven and cool on a wire rack.

7. To make the filling and topping, place sugar and water in a small saucepan, bring to the boil and boil for 10 minutes.

8. Whisk the yolks in a mixer and slowly pour sugar syrup into the yolks, whisking as you do so. Whisk until cool.

9. Fold in the butter and coffee. Sandwich the two cakes together with the filling and spoon the remaining mixture on top of the cake. Garnish with the halved walnuts.

ANNEKA RICE

TV Presenter

Orange Fairy Cakes

~METHOD~

1. Preheat oven to 180°C/350°F/Gas 4 and fill 2x12-hole fairy cake tins with paper cases.

2. Whisk the butter and sugar together in a bowl until light and fluffy.

3. Add the eggs one at a time with a tablespoon of flour per egg.

4. Fold in the rest of the flour.

5. Pour mixture carefully into the paper cases.

6. Bake the cakes for 15–20 minutes or until they are golden brown on top. Set aside to cool for 10 minutes on a wire rack before removing from the tin.

7. To make the icing, beat the cream cheese in a large bowl until soft and add half of the icing sugar and beat until smooth.

8. Add the remaining icing sugar and one tablespoon of orange or lime juice and beat until creamy. Beat in more juice if the icing needs softening.

9. Once the cakes are cool, spread the cream cheese icing on top of the cakes.

10. Decorate the cakes with grated orange or lime peel.

INGREDIENTS

SPONGE

- 4 free-range eggs

- 225g caster sugar

- 225g self-raising flour

- 225g butter, softened

ICING

- 110g cream cheese, softened

- 170g icing sugar

- Zest of an orange or lime

- 1-2 tbsp orange/lime juice

TO DECORATE

- Grated orange/lime peel

ANNABEL KARMEL

Bestselling author on baby food and nutrition

Heart Shaped Strawberry Cheesecakes

The ingredients work just as well as one larger cheesecake, cut into slices

~ METHOD ~

1. Halve the strawberries and place in a saucepan with the caster sugar and water. Simmer over a low heat until soft and the sugar has dissolved. Pass the mixture through a sieve into a bowl and leave to cool a little.

2. Meanwhile, soak the gelatine leaves in cold water for about 5 minutes. Squeeze any water from the gelatine, then add to the warm strawberry juice, stir until dissolved. Leave to cool completely.

3. To make the base, put the biscuits into a freezer bag and crush using a rolling pin then mix with the melted butter and spoon into the bases of four heart shaped springform tins. Press the biscuits firmly into the bases.

4. Put the cream cheese and vanilla extract into a mixing bowl. Slowly add the cold strawberry mixture and whisk until smooth, then carefully spoon the mixture into the tins. Transfer to the fridge and leave to set for about 4 hours or as long as possible.

5. Decorate with extra strawberries on top.

INGREDIENTS

- 350g strawberries

- 200g caster sugar

- 2 tbsp water

- 5 leaves gelatine

- 400g full fat cream cheese

- 1 tsp vanilla essence

- Biscuit Base:

- 100g digestive biscuits

- 50g butter, melted

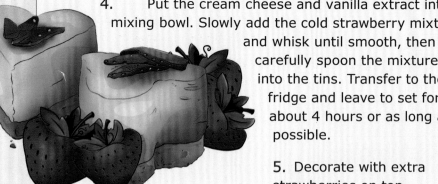

Recipe taken from "Cook It together" Dorling Kindersley annabelkarmel.com

SIAN LLOYD
TV Weather Presenter

Bryn's Spice Cake

This is brilliant fresh or toasted & buttered. You can also use the toasted crumbs as a base for puddings or just sprinkle them on yogurt or ice-cream.

INGREDIENTS

- 150ml/5fl oz milk
- 150g golden syrup
- 1 tsp bicarbonate of soda
- 100g caster sugar
- 100g soft dark brown sugar
- 130g softened butter
- 1 egg
- 280g plain flour
- 1 tsp ground cinnamon
- 1 tsp ground ginger

METHOD

1. Preheat oven to 160°C/325°F/Gas 3.

2. Line a 450g/1lb loaf tin with greaseproof paper.

3. Bring the milk & golden syrup to simmering point over a low heat. Remove from the heat, add the bicarbonate of soda and put to one side.

4. In a large bowl or using a food processor, cream both the sugars and butter together until pale and fluffy and add the egg, beating well.

5. Sift flour, cinnamon and ginger together and gently fold into the creamed mixture. Pour in the warm milk mixture combining well.

6. Pour mixture into tin and bake for 40 minutes. Leave in tin for 10 minutes. When done, turn out onto wire rack to cool completely.

Recipe taken from "Bryn's Kitchen" by Bryn Williams, published by Kyle Books.

MICHAEL CAINES MBE

Chef/Restaurateur

Carrot Cake with White Chocolate Ice Cream

Simple to make as individual desserts or a whole cake in a 260mm/10¼" diameter cake tin.

INGREDIENTS

EQUIPMENT:

- Round cake tin 260mm or 10¼"
- 12 hole cake tin
- Carrot Cake mixture
- 450ml/16fl oz vegetable oil (A)
- 400g plain flour (A)
- 10g bicarbonate of soda (A)
- 570g sugar (A)

- 290g eggs or 5 whole (A)
- Pinch of salt (A)
- 12g ground cinnamon (A)
- 530g carrots
- 150g walnuts

TOPPING

- 200g cream cheese
- 150g sugar
- 100g butter

WHITE CHOCOLATE ICE CREAM

- 1 litre/1¾ pints milk
- 100g sugar
- 10 egg yolks
- 400g white chocolate, melted on a bain-marie
- 55g milk powder
- 200ml/7fl oz double cream

~ METHOD ~

1. Mix the (A) ingredients in a mixer for 5 minutes. Grate the carrots and chop the nuts, then add them to the mix. If opting for individual cakes, equally portion the mixture into the compartments. If making one large cake, place mixture into 260mm diameter cake tin. Bake at 160°C/325°F/Gas 3 for approx 1¼ hours, check to see if the cake(s) are cooked then remove from the oven and allow to cool for 10 minutes in their tin(s) before removing and placing onto a cooling rack.

TOPPING

1. Place the cream cheese, sugar and butter into a mixing bowl and cream together until smooth and soft. Spread over the cakes using a palette knife. Alternatively, if making with children, place the topping into a piping bag and allow them to pipe the topping onto the individual cakes for an element of fun and individuality!

WHITE CHOCOLATE ICE CREAM

1. Cream together the egg yolks and the sugar until white and stiff. In a saucepan combine the milk, milk powder and cream, and bring to the boil. Pour some of the milk onto the creamed eggs and sugar, whisking continuously. Return the mixture to the saucepan and over a medium heat cook out to 85°C. Pass through a sieve and then pour in the melted white chocolate.

2. Turn in ice cream machine. Remove and place into the freezer.

3. Simply serve each individual cake with a scope of white chocolate ice cream.

4. A great way to introduce children to vegetables with a twist! You can disguise the fact that they are eating a vegetable with these simple, individual carrot cakes.

LESLEY NICOL

Actress (Mrs Patmore, Cook in Downton Abbey)

Vanilla Sponge

INGREDIENTS

SPONGE

- 4 eggs
- 125g/4½ oz caster sugar
- 115g/4oz self-raising flour

CUSTARD

- 1 tbsp cornflour
- 1 dstsp caster sugar
- ½ pt full-fat milk
- Knob of butter
- 1½ tsp vanilla extract
- 1 egg, beaten
- Double cream

TOPPING

- Icing sugar

METHOD

1. Line and grease two 18x18cm/7x7in cake tins. Beat the eggs and sugar well, and fold in the flour. Pour the mixture into the two baking tins. Bake at 170°C/325°F/Gas 3 for 20 minutes.

2. Mix the cornflour with a small amount of the milk to make a paste (quite loose). Put aside.

3. Put a bowl over a saucepan of boiling water. Put the milk, sugar and butter in the bowl and stir until melted. Pour this mixture onto the paste mixture, mix together and then put over the saucepan of boiling water and reheat until it's thick like a custard. Take it off the heat and let it cool for few minutes. Add the beaten egg into the custard, put it back over saucepan of boiling and reheat it for a it has thickened Add the vanilla extract and stir it in.

4. Leave to cool and when it has gone cold beat in some double cream and sandwich between the two sponges.

5. Sift some icing sugar into a bowl and add some water to make a paste.

6. Spread it on top of the cake and sprinkle some toasted almond slivers on top.

7. Delicious!

Winner, The Great British Bake Off 2010

Lemon Yogurt and Cherry Cake

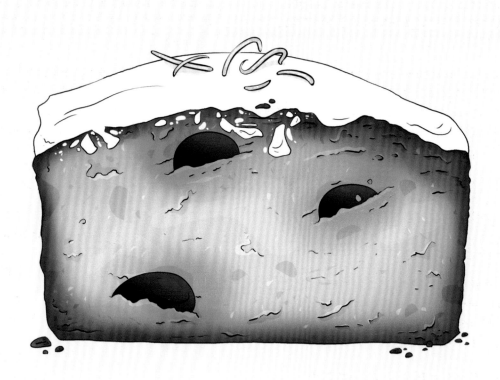

Recipe from *The Boy Who Bakes*

~INGREDIENTS~

- 225g plain flour
- 2 tsp baking powder
- ½ tsp salt
- 175ml/6fl oz lemon yoghurt (plain will work too)
- 200g golden caster sugar

- 3 large eggs
- Zest of 1 lemon
- ½ tsp vanilla extract
- 150g unsalted butter, melted and cooled
- 150g cherries pitted and quartered

FROSTING

- 100g unsalted butter, room temperature
- 200g icing sugar
- ½ tsp vanilla extract
- 80g lemon curd
- 1 tbsp milk

~METHOD~

1. Grease and line a standard loaf pan and pre-heat the oven to 180°C/160°C Fan/350°F/Gas 4.

2. In a medium bowl mix the flour, baking powder and salt together. In a large bowl mix together until combined the yoghurt, sugar, eggs, lemon zest, vanilla extract and butter.

3. Sift the flour mixture over the liquid ingredients and gently fold together (don't beat or the cake will be tough) until the dry ingredients are incorporated.

4. Lightly dust the cherries with about ½ tbsp flour, which will help the cherries from sinking in the cake, then lightly mix into the batter.

5. Pour into the prepared loaf pan and lightly level out. Bake for 60–65 minutes or until a toothpick inserted into the middle of the cake comes out clean.

6. Allow to cool in the pan for 15 minutes before removing to cool completely on a wire rack.

7. To make the frosting beat the butter in an electric mixer fitted with the paddle until very pale then slowly incorporate the icing sugar and beat until light and fluffy. Add the lemon curd, vanilla extract and milk and beat until combined. Spread across the cake and serve.

TRACY-ANN OBERMAN

Actress

Old Style Cheesecake

This very old family recipe is from my late grandmother for Cheese Cake which is from her mother before her: it's old style measurements I'm afraid but hence it's meaningful to me. It's written in her scrawly handwriting in an old notebook that dates back to the early 50s. Family memories are important!

INGREDIENTS

- 1lb cooking cheese
- Half a glass of sugar
- Juice of one lemon
- 2 eggs

~ METHOD ~

1. Mix all the ingredients.

2. Spoon over crushed digestive biscuit for base.

3. Cook for half an hour at 180°C/350°F/Gas 4.

4. Add 2 cartons of sour cream.

5. 1 dessert spoon of sugar.

6. 1 drop of vanilla essence.

7. Cook for a further 10 minutes.

8. Turn off oven and leave to set.

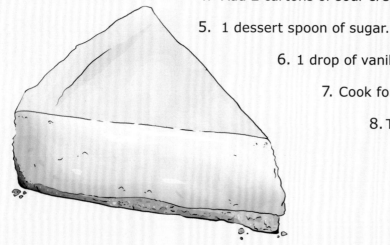

IMOGEN EDWARDS-JONES

Journalist/Broadcaster/Novelist

Mini Banana Muffins

~ METHOD ~

1. Pre-heat oven to 180°C/350°F/Gas 4.

2. Mix the egg and the sugar together in a large bowl. Add the vanilla extract and beat until thick.

3. Mash the banana and add to the mixture.

4. Add oil and mix well.

5. Sieve the floor, cinnamon, bicarbonate of soda, baking powder and salt into the mixture, adding the remanding bran left in the sieve.

6. Mix until it is all combined together and then place into small paper cases in a muffin tin. Only fill two-thirds and if you fancy place a slice of banana on top.

7. Place in the oven and cook for 12–14 minutes.

INGREDIENTS

- 1 egg
- 55g soft brown sugar
- 1 soft large ripe banana
- 55ml sunflower oil
- 85g wholemeal flour
- ½ tsp baking powder
- ½ tsp bicarbonate of soda
- ½ tsp ground cinnamon
- ½ tsp vanilla extract
- Pinch of salt

LOTTE DUNCAN

Food Network UK Cook

Squidgy Pear and Ginger Cake

INGREDIENTS

MAKES ONE 23CM/9IN CAKE

- Butter, for greasing
- 1 heaped tablespoon demerara sugar
- 4 medium sized pears, peeled, cored and cut into quarters
- 225g butter, softened
- 225g soft brown sugar
- Grated zest of ½ orange
- 4 large eggs
- 175g self-raising flour, sieved
- ½ tsp baking powder
- 1 tsp ground ginger
- 50g ground almonds
- 1 lump of preserved ginger (in syrup), finely chopped

METHOD

1. Preheat the oven to 180°C/Fan 160°C/Gas 4.

2. Grease and line a 23cm/9in spring-form cake tin.

3. Scatter the demerara sugar over the bottom of the cake tin and then arrange the pear quarters in a circular pattern on top.

4. Cream the butter, sugar and orange zest together in a medium mixing bowl, using a wooden spoon or electric whisk, until pale and fluffy.

5. Beat the eggs into the creamed mixture, one at a time. Add 1 teaspoon of flour to the mixture between each addition. This is quite a runny cake mixture so don't worry. It might even look a bit curdled, but it's absolutely fine.

6. Using a metal spoon, fold in the rest of the flour, the baking powder, ground ginger, ground almonds and the preserved ginger and pour the mixture over the pears in the cake tin.

7. Spread the mixture evenly in the tin and bake for 30 minutes. Then remove, cover loosely with foil and continue to cook for another 30 minutes.

8. Remove the cake from the oven and leave it to cool for 5 minutes in the tin and then turn it out onto a wire rack.

TARA FLYNN

Actress

I Can't Believe It's Not (Got) Butter...or Eggs... Lemon/Lime Cake

I've been vegan for 4 years now, and the only downside is the lack of readily available egg-and-dairy free cake. Particularly egg-and-dairy-free cake that doesn't taste like it's been swept up from the floor of a carpenter's workshop, or like it's been invented by a very serious doctor. A very, very serious, healthy, boring doctor. Many vegans spend a lot of time talking about baking and cakes and the moistness and delicious-ness thereof. This is one of the moister and deliciouser kind. Also, it's dead easy and you can make it in cupcake form if you prefer (just remember to bake them for a shorter time – about 15–20 mins.) Hope you enjoy!

~♥ INGREDIENTS ♥~

FOR THE CAKE:

- 2 large lemons (or limes)

- 2 tbsp lime zest (2 or 3 limes)

- 1½ cups plain flour

- 1 cup demerara sugar

- 1 tsp bicarbonate of soda

- 5 tbsp sunflower oil

- 1 tsp vinegar

- 1 tsp vanilla

- 3/4 cup water

FOR THE ICING:

- 2 tbsp lemon or lime juice

- ¾ cup icing sugar

~♥ METHOD ♥~

FOR THE CAKE:

1. Use a 20cm/8in round tin. Mix together flour, demerara sugar and bicarbonate of soda in a bowl.

2. Grate lime until you have 2 tbsp of zest.

3. Juice lemon for 3 tbsp of juice. Mix juice with water (in separate bowl from flour mix).

4. To that add the oil, vanilla and vinegar. Mix very well.

5. Then pour the wet ingredients mixture into the flour and whisk well. Keep whisking, even if it foams a bit!

6. Pour into baking dish & bake for 25 minutes at 180°C/350°F/Gas 4

THEN, FOR THE ICING:

1. Wait for the cake(s) to cool.

2. Juice more lemons and/or limes until you have 2 tbsp of juice.

3. Then mix with the icing sugar and pour on top of the (cool) cake.

4. Let it rest for about an hour if you'd like the icing to harden or –to hell with it - just go for it and tuck in while the icing is soft.

BRIAN TURNER

TV Chef/Author

Lily's Ginger Cake

Lily's ginger cake is a recipe from Brian's mother which has been passed down.

~ INGREDIENTS ~

- **Makes:** 8 good portions
- 225g unsalted butter
- 280g sugar
- 3 tbsp golden syrup

- 1½ cups boiling water
- 450g self-raising flour
- 3 tsp ground ginger
- 2 tsp bicarbonate of soda in a little milk

BUTTER CREAM

- 225g unsalted butter
- 175g icing sugar
- 115g drained crystallized ginger

~ METHOD ~

1. Melt butter, sugar and syrup in water.

2. Remove from the heat, add sieved flour and ginger.

3. Add milk/ bicarbonate mixture in and quickly beat well.

4. Put into an 20cm/8" cake tin, greased and floured or lined.

5. Bake at 170°C/325°F/ Gas 3 for approx 45 minutes.

6. Take out and sit for five minutes then put onto a cooling rack to cool.

7. This cake is better if left to stand in an airtight tin, not in fridge for 24 hours then make butter cream.

8. Sieve icing sugar carefully.

9. Cream the butter and sugar together, add chopped ginger.

10. Cut the cake in half horizontally and use the icing to sandwich the cake and also spread a little on top.

PAUL RANKIN

TV Chef/Author

Poppyseed Teacake

INGREDIENTS

MAKES ONE BUNDT TIN MOLD

- 125g unsalted butter
- 375g sugar
- 2 eggs
- 350g plain flour
- 1½ tsp bicarbonate of soda
- 125 ml/4fl oz sour cream
- 250ml/9fl oz water
- 125g white chocolate, finely chopped (or pulsed in food processor)
- ¼ cup poppy seeds
- 1 tbsp orange zest

~ METHOD ~

1. Oven at 180°C/350°F/Gas 4.

2. Cream butter and sugar until light and fluffy.

3. Add sifted dry ingredients alternately with sour cream, orange zest and water.

4. Lastly fold in white chocolate and poppy seeds.

5. Into a medium oven. Bake for 1–1½ hours at 180°C/350°F/Gas 4.

6. When cool glaze with following glaze.

7. 60g white chocolate, melted.

8. 2 tbsp orange juice.

9. 1 cup icing sugar, sifted.

10. Mix well to get a nice, glaze consistency.

LAURA HAMILTON

Presenter of A Place in the Sun on Channel 4, Fort Boyard on ITV1 and finalist on Dancing On Ice 2011 on ITV1

Non-Bake Baileys and Oreo Cheesecake

It's boozy, thick, creamy and yummy. I made this recently when some friends came over for dinner and it went down a treat!

INGREDIENTS

MAKES ONE 8-IN ROUND CHEESECAKE TO SERVE 8 PEOPLE

- 200g Oreo cookies, after the cream centre is removed

- 100g butter, melted

- 200ml whipping cream

- 150ml Bailey's Irish Cream

- 4 teaspoons gelatine

- 500g cream cheese, softened at room temperature

- 130g caster sugar (use up to 150g if you prefer a sweeter cake)

- 50g melted dark chocolate

METHOD

1. Using a food processor, process the Oreo cookies until they are fine crumbs.

2. Add the melted butter into the cookie crumbs and stir until they are all combined. Transfer into one 20cm/8in round pan (preferably with a loose bottom), pressing it down to form an even layer over the bottom of the pan. Freeze the crust layer while you prepare the remaining ingredients.

3. Whip the cream until it's firm. Then pop in the fridge.

4. Place the Bailey's into a small bowl. Sprinkle the gelatine evenly over the surface of the Baileys and let stand for 2–3 minutes. Place the small bowl in a pot of simmering water and heat gently, stirring constantly until the gelatine has dissolved and the mixture is smooth.

5. Using an electric mixer, beat the cream cheese and the sugar until light and fluffy. Strain the gelatine mixture into the cream cheese mixture and mix together gently. Fold in the whipped cream gently. Pour onto your biscuit base, don't bother smoothing the surface if you are going to do a chocolate decoration.

6. Scoop dollops of the melted dark chocolate over the cream cheese mixture. Using a skewer or a tooth pick, swirl decorations on the cheesecake.

7. Refrigerate the cheesecake for a minimum of 4 hours, but ideally overnight.

8. When ready to serve: dip a palette knife into hot water and dry it. Run the knife along the edges of the cheesecake and remove the pan carefully and gently. Place it on a serving plate and eat!

MICH TURNER MBE

Baker/Patron of

Little Venice Cake Company

Queen Elizabeth Date Cake

Melting, moist and tasty, this nutritious cake is sustaining and simple to make, and it turns out well every time. It can be covered with marzipan and sugar paste and decorated for an impressive centre-piece, or simply enjoyed on its own served with English breakfast tea or some freshly brewed coffee.

~ INGREDIENTS ~

- 200g unsalted butter, cut into pieces, plus extra for greasing

- 240g Medjool dates, stoned

- 50g sultanas

- 300g light brown sugar

- 2 eggs, lightly beaten

- 25g preserved stem ginger, chopped

- Grated zest of 2 lemons

- 1 tsp vanilla extract

- 250g Bramley cooking apples, peeled and cored, then grated or chopped

- 200g plain flour

- ½ tsp baking powder

~ METHOD ~

1. Fan 150°C/300°F.

2. Conventional 170°C/325°F/ Gas 3.

3. Preheat the oven. Grease and line a deep 15cm/6in round cake tin or 900g/2lb loaf tin with non-stick baking paper, or use a non-stick tin. Ensure all the ingredients are at room temperature.

4. Place the dates and sultanas in a bowl and cover with boiling water. Melt the butter and light brown sugar together in a saucepan and leave to cool slightly. Beat the eggs, ginger, lemon zest and vanilla extract into the butter and sugar. Drain the fruit and chop the dates finely. Add to the saucepan with the apples and mix well. Sift in the flour and baking powder and fold in well.

5. Spoon the mixture into the tin and bake in the oven for about 1¼ hours until well risen and a skewer inserted into the middle of the cake comes out clean. Leave to cool in the tin.

TO STORE

This cake lasts for 1 week if wrapped in greaseproof paper and aluminium foil stored in an airtight container. Alternatively, wrap the cake in a double layer of greaseproof paper and aluminium foil and place in the freezer for up to 1 month. It is delicious if kept in the fridge and served cold.

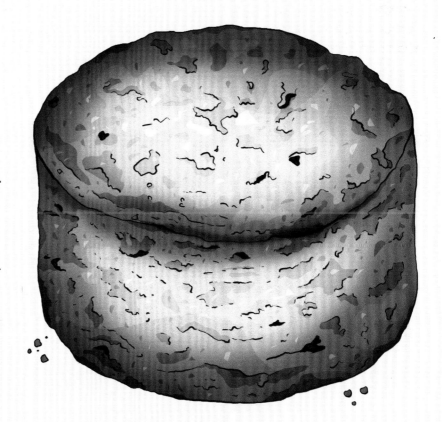

EMMA FORBES

TV/Radio Presenter

Lemon Squares

A wonderfully zesty treat

~ INGREDIENTS ~

MAKES 16

PREP/COOKING

- 15 mins/30 mins

FOR THE BASE

- 100g unsalted butter, at room temperature
- 40g icing sugar
- 150g plain flour
- 3 tbsp milk

FOR THE TOPPING

- 3 medium eggs
- 220g caster sugar
- Grated zest of 2 lemons and juice of 1 lemon
- 40g icing sugar, for dusting

Text © Emma Forbes taken from
Life & Soul, published by Ivy Press,
ISBN: 978-1-907332-86-9

METHOD

TO MAKE THE LEMON SQUARES

1. Preheat the oven to 180°C/350°F/Gas 4. Line a shallow 20cm/ 8in square cake tin with baking paper.

2. To make the base, in an electric mixer, or using a large mixing bowl and an electric hand-held mixer, cream the butter and sugar together.

3. Add the flour and then the milk and mix together until smooth. Spoon the mixture into the prepared tin, spreading it over the base and working it into the corners of the tin.

4. Bake in the oven for 15 minutes.

5. Meanwhile, make the topping. In a clean electric mixer or another bowl, whisk the eggs and sugar together until light and fluffy.

6. Add the lemon zest and juice and then fold in the flour.

7. Remove the cooked bottom layer from the oven and spoon the lemon mixture on top.

8. Return to the oven and bake for a further 15 minutes, until golden. Leave in the tin to cool completely.

9. To serve, cut into 16 squares and dust with sifted icing sugar.

KRISTINA RIHANOFF

Professional Dancer on
Strictly Come Dancing

Banana Loaf

INGREDIENTS

- 225g self-raising flour
- Pinch of salt
- ¼ tsp mixed spice
- 115g margarine
- 450g ripe bananas
- 175g sugar
- 175g mixed fruit
- 55g chopped walnuts
- 2 beaten eggs

METHOD

1. Grease and line a loaf tin with baking paper.

2. Pre-heat the oven to 180°C/350°F/Gas 4.

3. Sieve flour, spice and salt into a bowl.

4. Rub in margarine until mixture resembles fine bread crumbs.

5. Peel bananas and mash with sugar, add to flour mix. Combine with all the other ingredients and mix well.

6. Turn into the prepared loaf tin.

7. Bake in the middle of the oven for approximately 1 hour.

8. Turn onto a wire rack to cool.

© James Steen

MARCO PIERRE WHITE

TV Chef/Restaurateur

Really Easy Cheesecake

INGREDIENTS

SERVES 6

- 1 egg
- 1 vanilla pod, scraped
- 800g full fat soft cheese.
- 65g butter, melted
- 115g packet digestive biscuits, crushed
- 115g caster sugar
- 115g crème fraiche

~ METHOD ~

1. Pre-heat the oven to 160°C/325°F/Gas 3.

2. In a large mixing bowl, blend together the crème fraîche, full fat soft cheese, eggs, the seeds of the vanilla pod and sugar.

3. Make the base of the cake by mixing the melted butter with the crushed biscuits.

4. Place the crushed biscuit mixture in the bottom of a baking tin. Layer the cheese mixture on top of the biscuit base.

5. Bake for 20 minutes in the oven (the cheesecake should not colour during cooking). How easy is that?

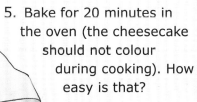

CAKES 85

GARY RHODES OBE

TV Chef/Restaurateur

Black Cherry
Victoria Sponge Cake

～ INGREDIENTS ～

A splash of Amaretto liqueur stirred into the cherry cream enriches the flavour of the cherries.

SERVES 8

- 175g self-raising flour

- 1 level tsp baking powder

- 175g butter, at room temperature, plus extra for greasing

- 175g caster sugar

- Grated zest of 1 orange or 1 lemon

- A few drops of vanilla essence

- 3 eggs, at room temperature

- Milk, to loosen

- Icing sugar, for dusting

FOR THE FILLING

- 150ml (5fl oz) double cream

- 200g black cherry jam

～ METHOD ～

1. Preheat the oven to 170°C/325°F/Gas 3. Lightly grease two 20cm (8in) in diameter and 2.5cm (1in) deep cake tins with a little butter and line the bottoms with greaseproof paper.

2. Sift the flour and baking powder into a bowl. Put the butter, caster sugar, zest and vanilla essence in another bowl and, using an electric hand whisk, beat together for 1–2 minutes until light and creamy. Add the eggs one at a time and beat until totally combined. Fold in the flour. The mixture should drop off a spoon easily, but if it is too thick, loosen with a little milk.

3. Divide the mixture between the two tins, smoothing the tops.

4. Bake in the centre of the oven for 20–25 minutes. To check the sponges are cooked, press your finger gently on top and the imprint should spring back. If it doesn't, bake for a further 5 minutes.

5. Remove the cakes from the oven and leave to rest for a few minutes, then run a knife around the edges, turning the cakes out on to a wire rack. Remove the greaseproof paper and leave to cool completely.

6. Whip the double cream to a soft peak and fold in the cherry jam. Spread the cherry cream over one of the sponges and sit the other sponge on top, then dust with icing sugar.

HAYLEY OKINES

Progeria sufferer and author of

Old Before My Time

Fairy Cakes

INGREDIENTS

MAKES 12

- 100g soft butter
- 100g self-raising flour
- 100g caster sugar
- 2 eggs

ICING

- 175g icing sugar
- Water

∽ METHOD ∽

1. Pre-heat oven to 180°C/350°F/Gas 4.

2. Whisk all the ingredients until creamy and smooth.

3. Spoon into fairy cake cases in a fairy cake tin.

4. Bake for 10–15 minutes until cooked.

5. If cooked, they should spring back gently when touched.

6. Mix icing sugar with some water until it makes a paste and spread it on the cooled cakes. Decorate with sprinkles, sweets, fruit, etc.

MIRIAM GONZALEZ DURANTEZ

Lawyer and wife of Liberal Democrat party leader, Nick Clegg

Olive Oil Cake

"I am a fan of olive oil. As this recipe shows it can be used not only for savories but also for cakes. Its distinctive strong smell and complex flavour will take you straight into the Mediterranean when baking this cake."

INGREDIENTS

- 4 eggs
- 175g/6oz sugar
- 150ml/5fl oz olive oil
- 145g/5oz plain flour
- Pinch of salt
- 1 tbsp baking powder
- Grated zest of 1½ lemons
- 2 tbsp pine nuts

METHOD

1. Preheat the oven at 175°C/325°F/Gas 3.

2. Beat the eggs and the sugar with an electric mixer or by hand until the mixture looks pale.

3. Add the olive oil and continue mixing (add the oil in little bits as otherwise the mixture could curdle).

4. Add the lemon zest.

5. Separately mix the flour, salt and baking powder, sift it and fold it into the mixture so that you do not lose the air.

6. Put it all in a greased mould (no need to line it).

7. Sprinkle the pine nuts on top and bake in the oven for 40-45 minutes.

ERIC LANLARD

Chef

Lemon Meringue Cupcakes

These cuties are a mixture between a lemon sponge cake and a lemon meringue pie.

INGREDIENTS

MAKES 12 MUFFINS

- Preparation time: 20 minutes

- Cooking time: 15–20 minutes

FOR THE CUPCAKES

- 100g unsalted butter, softened

- 100g caster sugar

- 1 vanilla pod, split

- 2 eggs

- 100g self-raising flour, sifted

- Finely grated zest of 1 lemon

- 75g good quality ready-made or home-made lemon curd

FOR THE MERINGUE

- 2 egg whites

- 100g caster sugar

METHOD

1. Preheat the oven to 180°C (Fan 160°C)/350°F/Gas 4. Line a 12-cup muffin tin with cupcake papers.

2. For the cupcakes, cream the butter, sugar and vanilla seeds together in a large mixing bowl, using an electric hand whisk, until pale, fluffy and well combined.

3. Crack in the eggs, one at a time, and beat until both are fully incorporated into the mixture. Fold in the sifted flour and lemon zest until well combined.

4. Spoon the cupcake batter into the cupcake papers. Add 1 tsp of lemon curd to the top of each cupcake.

5. Bake the cupcakes in the preheated oven for 15-20 minutes, or until they are pale golden-brown and spring back when pressed lightly in the centre.

6. Meanwhile, for the meringue, whisk the egg whites until soft peaks form when the whisk is removed. Gradually add the sugar, whisking continuously, until stiff peaks form when the whisk is removed. The mixture should be thick and glossy.

7. When the cakes are cooked, turn off the oven and preheat the grill to its highest setting.

8. Spoon the meringue into a piping bag with a small plain tube and pipe some in a spiral on top of each cupcake. Place the cupcakes under the hot grill 2 minutes to colour (or you can use a kitchen blowtorch to toast the meringue).

Taken from Home Bake by Eric Lanlard, published by Mitchell Beazley

JONATHAN PHANG

Former judge on Britain's Next Top Model
Caribbean food expert on Market Kitchen

Black Cake

INGREDIENTS

CAKE

- 3 eggs
- 114g lightly salted butter
- 114g self-raising flour
- 150g caster sugar
- 2 tbsp dark rum

- 2 tbsp cherry brandy
- 350g good quality mixed fruit
- 114g glace cherries
- 1 tsp baking powder
- 2 tsp mixed essence

- 1 tsp vanilla essence
- 1 tsp almond essence
- 1 tsp mixed spice
- 450g demerara sugar

ICING (OPTIONAL)

- Guava jelly
- Marzipan
- Royal Icing

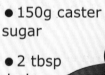

~ METHOD ~

1. Combine the mixed fruit and glace cherries. Take out one quarter of the mixed fruit and cherries (leaving fruit whole) and set aside in a deep jar. Roughly grind the remaining three quarters of the fruit and add to the whole fruit. Soak generously with equal measures of dark rum and cherry brandy. Add two teaspoons of mixed essence and one teaspoon of baking powder. Cover securely and leave in a cool dark place to steep for a minimum of three weeks or for up to a year.

2. (Should you not have the time to soak the fruit in advance, grind the fruit and cherries and place in a saucepan. Add two tablespoons of sugar, Dark Rum and Cherry Brandy. Bring to the boil and simmer until soft allow to cool before use.)

3. For the burnt sugar, place one pound of demerara sugar in a pan and heat until caramelised and gently bubbling add approximately 1 cup of boiling water gradually and stir well.

4. When the mixture is the colour and consistency of molasses remove from heat and cool in an empty jar.

5. In a deep mixing bowl chop butter in to cubes and let soften at room temperature. Add the sugar and beat until light and pale.

6. Add the eggs one at a time and mix well. Sift the self-raising flour and fold in to the batter in spoonfuls until smooth.

7. Flavour with mixed spice, vanilla and almond essence.

8. Pour in 2 tbsp burnt sugar and stir (the batter should now look dark brown).

9. Take the fruit out of the jar with a slotted spoon, drain and add to the batter.

10. Pour the cake batter into a greased and lined spring form baking tin (allow the greaseproof paper to be three inches higher that the top of the tin) and bake at 170°C for approximately 1½ hours.

11. Test if the cake is cooked by sticking a wooden skewer or cocktail stick into the centre of the cake, if it comes out clean the cake is cooked.

12. Remove the cake from the oven and leave to cool in the tin. Make several holes in the top of the cake and pour the dark rum and cherry brandy over the cake.

13. Wrap the top of the cake with the overlapping greaseproof paper and cover with foil. Leave for at least 24 hours for the alcohol to be absorbed.

14. Remove the black cake from the tin and brush it all over with a thin layer of melted guava jelly, cover with marzipan and royal icing.

15. Enjoy!

STACEY SOLOMON

Singer/TV Presenter

Pink Strawberry Cheesecake

⟡ INGREDIENTS ⟡

FOR THE BASE

- 200g digestive biscuits

- 100g unsalted butter, melted

FOR THE FILLING

- 3 sheets leaf gelatine

- 142 ml carton single cream

- 300g full-fat soft cheese

- 100g golden caster sugar

- Finely grated zest of half a lemon

- 3 tbsp lemon juice

- 300g chopped strawberries

- 142 ml carton double cream

- 1 medium egg white

FOR THE SAUCE

- 250g chopped strawberries + a few extra to decorate the top

- Finely grated zest of half a lemon

- 3 tbsp lemon juice

- 2 tbsp golden caster sugar

～ METHOD ～

1. Put the biscuits in a plastic bag and crush them into fine crumbs with a rolling pin. Tip into a bowl and stir in the melted butter, mixing thoroughly. Now tip the mixture into a greased loose-bottomed 24cm round cake tin, at least 5cm deep, and press down with the back of a metal spoon to make an even layer over the bottom of the tin. Chill in the fridge while you make the filling.

2. Submerge the gelatine leaves in a dish of cold water, and leave to soak and soften for 5 minutes. Pour the single cream into a pan and bring just to the boil, then take off the heat. Take the gelatine leaves out of the water, give them a good squeeze to get rid of excess water, and stir one by one into the cream (they will dissolve instantly). Leave to cool for a few minutes.

3. Beat the cheese in a bowl with the sugar, lemon zest and juice until smooth and creamy. Mix in the cream and gelatine mixture and the chopped strawberries.

4. In another bowl, lightly whip the double cream so it falls in soft peaks, fold it into the strawberry mixture. Whisk the egg white in a clean bowl until it forms stiff peaks, then fold gently into the cheese mixture. Pour into the cake tin and smooth down lightly. Chill for at least 2½ hours until set.

5. To make the sauce, blitz all the ingredients in a food processor or blender. Taste and add more sugar if needed, then pour into a jug and keep in the fridge until you're ready to serve.

6. To serve, run a knife between the cheesecake and the tin to loosen it, remove it from the tin, then take it off its base and put it on a serving plate. Halve the extra strawberries lengthways, pile them in the middle and serve with the jug of sauce.

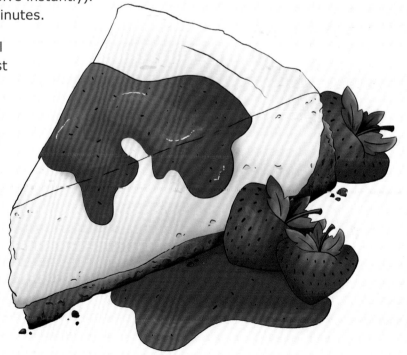

CHERIE LUNGHI

Actress

Aunty Biddy's Lemon Drizzle Cake

INGREDIENTS

- 140g self raising flour
- 115g caster sugar
- 115g margarine
- 2 eggs
- Zest of ½ Lemon
- 1 tbsp lemon curd
- ½ tsp baking powder (dissolved in 1 tbsp of hot water)
- 1 18x18cm/7x7in baking tin

LEMON GLAZE

- 1 Lemon
- 1 tbsp granulated sugar

～ METHOD ～

1. Beat margarine and sugar together.

2. Beat in the eggs and zest of ½ a lemon.

3. Fold in flour, lemon curd and dissolved baking powder.

4. Bake in oven 180°C/350°F/Gas 4 for 50 minutes.

TO MAKE THE GLAZE

1. Warm the juice of the lemon with the granulated sugar until the sugar has melted.

2. When the cake is done take it out of the oven and pour over the glaze immediately.

3. Leave the cake in the tin until it is cold, then remove from tin.

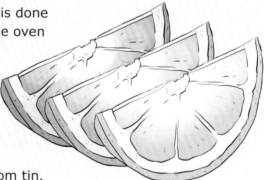

BISCUITS

MARY BERRY

Baker/Food Writer/Judge on
The Great British Bake Off

Double Chocolate Cookies

Dead easy to make, these are wonderful cookies. Expect an irregular shape. They are very soft when they come out of the oven but will harden up considerably on cooling. This recipe makes about 36 cookies.

~ METHOD ~

INGREDIENTS

● 200g plain chocolate (39% cocoa solids)

● 50g butter

● 397g can condensed milk

● 225g self-raising flour

● 65g milk chocolate or white chocolate buttons

1. Lightly grease 3 baking trays. Break up the chocolate and gently melt it along with the butter in a bowl set over a pan of simmering water, stirring occasionally. Stir in the condensed milk then take off the heat and cool.

2. Mix in the flour and the chocolate buttons and chill the mixture until firm enough to handle. Pre-heat the oven to 180°C/350°F/Gas 4.

3. Place large tspfuls of the mixture spaced well apart on the prepared baking trays. Bake in the pre-heated oven for about 15 minutes. The cookies should still look soft and will glisten.

4. Don't overcook them as they soon become very hard. Carefully remove the cookies with a palette knife and cool on a wire rack.

Photograph: Getty
Images ©

HER ROYAL HIGHNESS, THE DUCHESS OF CORNWALL

Sultana Flapjack Bars

INGREDIENTS

(MAKES 18)

- 450g plump sultanas
- ½ tsp mixed spice
- 300g light brown sugar
- 350g butter
- 300g rolled porridge oats
- 140g plain flour
- 3 tbsp golden syrup

METHOD

1. Heat the oven to 180°C (fan) or 200°C (conventional).

2. Place the sultanas, mixed spice, sugar, oats, flour and a pinch of salt into a large mixing bowl.

3. Melt the butter in a saucepan with the golden syrup and then add to the dry ingredients in the mixing bowl.

4. Grease a square baking tin of approximately 20x20cm with a little butter. Press the mixture into the tin and bake for 45 minutes until golden brown.

5. Leave to cool and then cut into 18 pieces. The flapjacks will keep for approximately two days.

GIVEN BY HER ROYAL HIGHNESS THE DUCHESS OF CORNWALL

RAYMOND BLANC OBE

Chef/Author/Restaurateur

Raspberry Macaroon

Macaroons are often the standard by which a good patisserie is measured. This recipe will unfold the little secrets of the macaroon and give you a huge satisfaction. You may need a little practice, but every mistake will still be delicious. Trust me, I know!

At the moment macaroons are the little black dress of cooking – another reason to make them yourself – and if not, buy them at Maison Blanc!

Here is a recipe that will allow you to match and sometimes exceed the quality of shop bought macaroons; for the simple reason they are fresh and you know all the ingredients that you put in to it.

These macaroons can be done in many different shapes and flavours – see chart at end of recipe.

~ INGREDIENTS ~

FOR THE PATÉ À MACAROON:

● 185g icing sugar

● 185g ground almonds

● 2 egg whites (70g) (*1)

● 25 drops natural red

food colouring

FOR THE FILLING:

● 140g raspberry jam, good quality or homemade

FOR THE ITALIAN MERINGUE:

● (Here I use a

Meringue Italian which gives better results than a Meringue Francaise)

● 75g egg whites

● Dash lemon juice (*2)

● 185g caster sugar

● 50g water

METHOD

FOR MAKING THE PATÉ À MACAROON:

1. Preheat your oven to 170°C with an oven tray on the middle shelf. (*3)

2. In a large bowl, mix the icing sugar, ground almond and the egg whites to form a paste. Then stir in the food colouring in 3 stages as some colourings will be stronger than others

FOR THE ITALIAN MERINGUE

1. In a mixing machine on medium speed, whisk the egg whites and a drop of lemon juice.

2. At the same time in a small saucepan on a high heat, cook the sugar with the water to 117°C or 'soft boil'.

3. Reduce the speed on the mixer to low (THIS IS CRITICAL as the hot syrup is dangerous and can burn if it makes contact with your skin) and pour the hot sugar syrup (*5) directly into the firmly whipped whites, increase the mixer speed to high and continue to whisk for 2-3 minutes. This makes what is called 'Italian Meringue'. This meringue is used in many many recipes such as Chiboust, Omelette Norvegienne, iced soufflé etc.

TO PIPE AND COOK THE MACAROONS:

1. Fold the warm (*5) Italian Meringue into the paté à macaroon mixture creating a ribbon stage (*6) ensuring that it is evenly mixed. (*7)

2. Place the nozzle in the piping bag, half fill with the mixture and pipe 3cm discs, (at least 2cm apart) (*8) onto baking trays lined with greaseproof paper. Slide the macaroons on the greaseproof paper onto the preheated tray and cook for 8 minutes.

3. Remove from the oven and leave to cool for 5 minutes on a cake cooling rack. Leave until room temperature before using.

TO FINISH:

1. Spoon approximately 1 teaspoon of raspberry jam onto the flat side of a macaroon and top with the flat side of a second macaroon like a sandwich. Repeat for the remaining macaroons.

2. Store as a single layer in a sealed container in the fridge until needed.

- **Serves (Yield):** 30 piece
- **Difficulty rating:** ●●○
- **Preparation time:** 30 min
- **Cooking time:** 12 min
- **Resting time:** 30 min for cooling
- **Special equipment:** Kitchen mixer, sugar thermometer, disposable piping bag with 8mm nozzle, hand blender
- **Planning ahead:** These are better made the day before and kept in the fridge in an airtight container as they will have a better texture. Frozen, they will improve as the crust will be the same and the inside will be moister and better textured. Just defrost 2-3 hours before.

～ CHEF'S NOTES ～

1. *Egg quality – Always buy organic or free range eggs. They follow good husbandry practices & good ethical standards. For all preparation where egg white is raw you must use an egg with the lion mark which comes from a vaccinated hen so you run no risk of salmonella.

2. Lemon Juice – just the smallest dash, 1 drop, is needed to prevent the graining of the egg white. Too much will completely stiffen the egg white and will make it impossible to fold in to your mixture.

3. Pre-heating the tray – by pre-heating the tray and placing the piped macaroons on this, you kick start the cooking and therefore create an extra rise – this forming a wonderful collar or "Collerette" as we would say at home. This not only gives the macaroons a very pleasing appearance, especially when sandwiched together, but also a wonderful firm texture and a great looking macaroon.

4. Sugar syrup - The sugar syrup needs to be this temperature in order to partially cook the whipped egg whites, the whites will effectively be poached and reach 65°C. REMEMBER to reduce the speed of the mixer and pour the syrup between the whisk and the bowl, so as to prevent the hot syrup from being sprayed out of the machine and potentially burning you.

5. Warm Meringue – if the meringue cools then it will be too stiff and will be hard to mix in to the almond mixture – creating an uneven batter and uneven macaroons.

6. Ribbon stage – this is the term that describes the consistency that the mix must achieve. To test this, take a spoon full of mix from the bowl and let it fall off the spoon back in to the bowl – it should sit on top of the mixture as a ribbon.

7. Over mixing – Be careful not to over mix as the result will be too liquid and harder to pipe – but you do need to knock a little of the air out as this will give your macaroons a more consistent denser finish, enhancing the chocolate colour and mouth feel. Fully over mixing the macaroons results in a cracked finish, where so much air has been knocked out that the shell is unstable and the fat in the almonds breaks down the mix's structure, making them become soft and runny. When cooked the mix will not form a stable shell and will therefore crack. Under mixing – by not mixing your ingredients well enough you will end up with a over light mix, producing macaroons with a large rise, but a pale, dull finish. The resulting macaroons do not have the same

beautiful dense texture or the rich deep colour as the properly mixed macaroons.

8. Piping - Don't pipe the macaroons too close together as they will expand slightly as they cook. Hold the piping bag vertically and always keep your hand tightly around the bag to keep a constant pressure.

VARIATIONS – COLOUR – FLAVOUR – FOR THE SAME QUANTITY AND COOKING TIME

1. **Lemon** – add 25 drops or 2.5g of yellow food colouring to the macaroon paste. For the filling 160g of lemon curd

2. **Chocolate** – fold 60g of melted chocolate (100%) to the paté à macaroon mixture.
For the filling, bring 100g of whipping cream to a simmer, take off the heat and stir in 100g of chocolate (65%)

3. **Pistachio** – Add 15 drops of green food colouring to the macaroon paste. For the filling 150g pistachio paste

4. **Vanilla** – leave the macaroon paste plain. Add 10g of vanilla puree to the macaroon paste. Filling – 150g of vanilla butter cream. You can do a frozen variation by using vanilla ice cream as a filling and keeping the macaroons in the freezer.

5. **Anise** – 4g of crushed star anise mixed in to the sugar and ground almonds, left to infuse overnight and then sieved out before making the paste. Filling – 150g of orange marmalade.

MACAROON CAKE

1. This macaroon can be served as the base of a cake and many other shapes can be created, such as tear drops, little hearts, fingers and of course the size can go from mini to large. Pipe 18cm diameter disc of macaroon mixture and bake as above.

2. Once cooled place a 16cm diameter pastry cake ring on top and cut off any excess.

3. Place the macaroon and cake ring on to a cake board or tray lined with greaseproof paper and pour in 400ml of chocolate delice filling (see recipe) and leave to set in the fridge overnight.

4. To serve gently heat the outside of the metal cake ring with a blow torch and remove.

5. Simply cut and serve to your guests, or you can decorate the outside with smaller chocolate macaroons.

EMILY MAITLIS

BBC Newsreader

Black and White Cookies

INGREDIENTS

- 100g plain flour
- 100g soft butter
- 100g porridge oats
- 100g golden caster sugar
- 100g dark, good chocolate broken into chunky irregular pieces
- 100g white good choc (ditto)
- 1 egg
- 1 tsp good vanilla essence
- 1 tsp baking powder

This is the easiest yummiest recipe for big fat American style cookies. The secret is to underbake so they are squidgey in the middle. And not to be stingy with the chocolate – you need large chunks not polka dots so it melts through the whole biscuit.

✤ METHOD ✤

1. Pre-heat oven to 190°C/375°F/Gas 5.

2. Cream the butter and sugar.

3. Add the egg and vanilla.

4. Add the porridge oats.

5. And sift the flour into mixture with baking powder. Stop when you have got something that resembles a sticky ball.

6. Add chunks of chocolate to mixture.

7. If it gets too dry add a touch of milk.

8. Take generous teaspoons of the mixture and place in balls onto a greased baking tray, well spaced apart.

9. Flatten with a fork and bake in oven for about 12–15 minutes or until they set and start to go golden but NOT too hard.

THE RT HON CAROLINE SPELMAN MP

Secretary of State for Environment, Food and Rural Affairs

Grasmere Gingerbread

INGREDIENTS

- 225g flour
- ½ tsp bicarbonate of soda
- Pinch of salt
- 1 level dstsp ground ginger
- 115g butter
- 1 tbsp golden syrup
- 115g soft brown sugar
- 55g candied peel or chopped dates

~ METHOD ~

1. Sieve flour, bicarbonate of soda, salt, ginger, and sugar.

2. Beat butter and syrup till creamy and then add the dry ingredients.

3. Add peel/dates. The mixture should be dry and crumbly but do not add liquid.

4. Press into well greased tin ½in deep and bake in slow oven 170°C/325°F/Gas 3 for 30–40 minutes.

5. Cut into squares while still warm but don't remove till cold.

 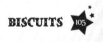

RICHARD CORRIGAN

Chef/Author/Restaurateur

Almond Rock Cake

INGREDIENTS

- 500g ground almonds
- 300g sugar
- 6 egg whites
- 1 tsp vanilla essence
- 50g flaked almonds

~ METHOD ~

1. Mix everything except the flaked almonds.

2. Divide into even/uneven shapes onto a baking tray.

3. Sprinkle with the flaked almonds.

4. Bake at 170°C/325°F/Gas 3 until golden.

5. Dust with icing sugar.

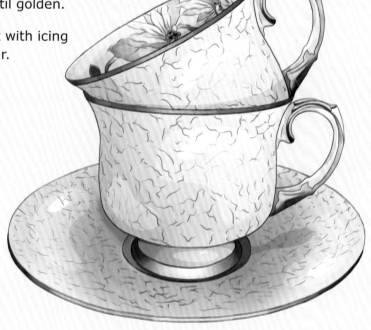

THE RT HON DAME TESSA JOWELL DBE MP

Shadow Minister for London
and the Olympics

All Day Breakfast Bars

(with thanks to Rachel)

INGREDIENTS

- 397g can sweetened condensed milk

- Walnut-sized knob of butter

- 250g rolled oats (not instant)

- 75g desiccated coconut

- 100g dried sour cherries, cranberries, prunes or apricots (or any other dried fruit in small pieces)

- 125g mixed seeds (a mixture of pumpkin, linseed, sunflower, sesame)

- 125g nuts (almonds, hazelnuts, macadamia or a mixture of any nuts you like)

- Pinch of salt

METHOD

1. Pre-heat oven to 140°C/275°F/Gas 1 and lightly grease a 25cmx25cm/10inx10in baking tin with a flavourless oil like sunflower.

2. Gently warm the condensed milk in a large pan, stir in the knob of butter until it melts and then add all the remaining ingredients, using a rubber spatula to mix up well.

3. Spread the mixture into the oiled tin and press down with a spatula or your hands (run quickly under the tap to stop you from sticking) to make the surface even.

4. Bake for 1 hour, then remove from oven, and after about 15 minutes, cut into squares or bars. Allow to cool completely and store in a tin.

MAKES ABOUT 16

YOTAM OTTOLENGHI AND SAMI TAMIMI

Chefs/Restaurateurs

Sour Cherry Amaretti

This is our version of the popular little Italian biscuit. Serve them with coffee or, even better, break them over chocolate ice cream. If you don't mind the effort, make your own ground almonds (blanch, peel and very lightly toast the almonds, then blitz them till they're fine). This will give a much deeper almond flavour. In any case, don't get carried away with the almond extract. Too much of it will give a terrible artificial aroma. You can omit the sour cherries if you wish, or use dried apricots or dried blueberries instead.

This recipe is taken from Ottolenghi: The Cookbook by Yotam Ottolenghi and Sami Tamimi (Ebury Press)

MAKES ABOUT 20

- 180g ground almonds

- 120g caster sugar

- Grated zest of 1 lemon

- 3 drops natural almond extract

- Pinch of salt

- 60g dried sour cherries, roughly chopped

- 2 free-range egg whites

- 2 tsp honey

- Plenty of icing sugar for rolling

~◦ METHOD ◦~

1. Preheat the oven to 170°C/325°F/ Gas 3. Put the ground almonds, sugar, lemon zest, almond extract and salt in a large bowl and rub with your fingertips to disperse the zest and essence evenly. Add the cherries and set aside.

2. Using a manual or electric whisk, beat the egg whites and honey until they reach a soft meringue consistency. Gently fold the meringue into the almond mixture. At this stage you should have a soft, malleable paste.

3. With your hands, form the mixture into 20 irregular shapes. Roll them in plenty of icing sugar, then arrange them on a baking tray lined with baking parchment. Place in the oven and bake for about 12 minutes.

4. The biscuits should have taken on some colour but remain relatively pale and chewy in the centre. Leave to cool completely before indulging, or storing them in a sealed jar.

TV Presenter

Shortbread

INGREDIENTS

- 200g plain flour

- 50g cornflour

- 175g unsalted softened butter

- 75g golden caster sugar

- Two 18x18cm/ 7x7in sandwich tins

- Food processor/ mixer

∽ METHOD ∾

1. Preheat oven to 180°C/350°F/Gas 4.

2. Whizz plain flour, cornflour, butter and sugar in the processor or mixer until it just comes together.

3. Take out and divide the dough into two pieces.

4. Lightly flour your work surface and roll into circles slightly smaller than 18x18cm/7x7in and then place in the two sandwich tins (thus the dough can spread out fully during baking, instead of bunching thickly into the corners and ending up a bit claggy).

5. Press the tines of a fork around the edges and then prick all over.

6. Bake for around 40 minutes, but as long as you can before it starts to overbrown – that way it will be beautifully short and melt-in-the-mouth.

7. When it's ready, sprinkle with caster sugar and cut into segments while hot.

ANDREW FAIRLIE

Chef Patron, Andrew Fairlie at
Gleneagles Hotel, Scotland

Peanut Butter Cookies

INGREDIENTS

- 250g softened butter

- 110g granulated sugar

- Pinch of salt

- 1 egg

- 225g plain flour

- 250g peanut butter

- 110g light brown sugar

- 4g baking powder

TO PREPARE DOUGH

1. Beat butter and salt, then add sugars, sifted flour and baking powder.

2. Add the egg, when the egg is incorporated add the peanut butter.

BAKING THE COOKIES

1. Shape the dough into rolls about 4cm in diameter and cut into 1cm slices.

2. Place the cookies onto a baking tray and place into a pre heated oven at 200°C/425°F/Gas 7 for 15 minutes.

3. The cookies should look slightly undercooked when finished.

4. Remove from tray and cool on a wire rack.

SIMON KING AND DAVE MYERS

The Hairy Bikers - TV Chefs

Norwegian Cardamom and Lemon Stamped Cookies

We discovered that cardamom is a really popular spice in Norway, used in many cake and biscuit recipes. Some say the spice was first brought back to the country hundreds of years ago by Vikings who worked as mercenaries in what was then Constantinople (now Istanbul). Whatever the truth, Norwegians are certainly keen on their cardamom.
We made these cookies on a boat on the Geiranger Fjord – a stunning spot.

INGREDIENTS

MAKES 24

- 225g butter, softened
- 150g caster sugar

- Finely grated zest of 1 lemon
- 250g plain flour
- 100g ground almonds

- 3 tsp ground cardamom or 1 heaped tsp cardamom seeds, ground in a pestle and mortar

⤳ METHOD ⤳

1. Preheat the oven to 190°C/Fan 170°C/Gas 5. Line 2 large baking trays with baking parchment.

2. Using an electric hand-whisk, beat the butter, sugar and lemon zest together in a large bowl until pale and fluffy. Beat in the flour, almonds and cardamom until the mixture is well combined and comes together to form a stiff dough.

3. Roll the dough into 24 balls and place 12 on each baking tray – make sure you leave space between each one. Press each cookie with a cookie stamp or the bottom of a glass to flatten and leave decorative indentations in the dough.

4. Bake a tray at a time for 12–14 minutes until the cookies are pale golden brown. Leave them to cool on the tray for a few minutes, then transfer to a wire rack. They will crisp up as they cool. Store the cookies in an airtight tin and eat within 7 days.

5. Tip: You can also make these cookies using a biscuit press. They'll be about half the size, so cook them for 10–12 minutes instead.

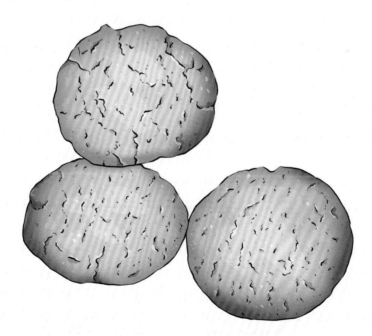

From The Hairy Bikers' Big Book of Baking published by Weidenfeld & Nicolson

TV Presenter

Fruit and Nut Biscotti

~INGREDIENTS~

- 310g plain flour

- Pinch of salt

- 225g caster sugar

- ½ tbsp baking powder

- 2 eggs

- 55g each of blanched almonds, pistachio nuts, chopped dried apricots and sultanas

- Zest of 1 lemon

GLAZE

- One beaten egg white

- Caster sugar

～ METHOD ～

1. Pre-heat oven to 350°F/180°C/Gas 4.

2. Line 2 baking sheets with parchment paper or non-stick baking paper.

3. In a large bowl or food processor, sift flour with salt and add caster sugar and baking powder.

4. Gradually add the eggs to make a soft dough.

5. Add the nuts, fruit and lemon zest and mix.

6. Divide the dough into 6 pieces and lightly dust work surface with flour and roll each piece to about 20cm/8in long and about 5cm/2in wide.

7. Place on baking sheets and brush each roll with the egg white and sprinkle with caster sugar.

8. Bake for 15 mins until firm.

9. Cut each biscotti on the angle into 1cm/½ in slices with a serrated knife.

10. Reduce the oven temperature to 275°F/140°C/Gas 1/Circo 130 and return the biscotti to the oven for 25–30 minutes.

11. Take out of oven and place on cooling racks.

12. When cold the biscotti will be lovely and crisp and ideal to serve with coffee after a meal.

13. OR they make wonderful gifts, presented in clear bags tied with a ribbon!

HARRIET SCOTT

Co-host radio presenter of the Breakfast show on London's Heart radio station

Oat Biscuits

These are biscuits I've made with my two-year-old, Louis.

~ METHOD ~

1. Pre-heat oven to 180°C/350°F/Gas 4 (160°C fan).

2. In a large mixing bowl, cream together the butter and caster sugar.

3. Sift the flour and fold in, followed by the oats, baking powder, vanilla essence, golden syrup and water.

4. The mixture should be quite firm, leaving the sides of the bowl when kneaded. Now you can add raisins or broken up pieces of chocolate.

5. Grease 2 baking sheets. Divide the mixture in to about 20 small balls, then flatten them slightly. Space them out well as they will spread as they cook.

6. After about 8 minutes they should look pale gold and a bit crispy round the edges.

7. Put them on a wire rack to cool and harden or munch after a few minutes while still warm!

INGREDIENTS

- 220g unsalted butter

- 175g caster sugar

- 225g self-raising flour

- 110g porridge oats

- ½ tsp baking powder

- A few drops vanilla essence (optional)

- 2 tsp golden syrup

- 2 tsp boiling water

ITV Weather Forecaster

Sienna's Party Biscuits

My daughter loves these and helps me make them

INGREDIENTS

- 111g butter, softened (plus extra for greasing)

- 115g brown sugar

- 1 tbsp golden syrup

- ½ tsp vanilla essence

- 175g self raising flour

- 85g smarties or choc chips

METHOD

1. Beat butter and sugar until light and fluffy, then beat in syrup and vanilla essence.

2. Sift half flour and work it into the mixture.

3. Add smarties or choc chips and the rest of the flour and work into a dough.

4. Roll out dough into 16 balls and place on prepared baking sheets, spaced well apart – do not flatten.

5. Bake in a preheated oven 180°/350°F/Gas 4 for 10–12 minutes.

6. Remove from oven and cool for 2 mins on baking sheets before transferring to wire racks to cool completely.

CARRIE GRANT

Vocal Coach/Singer/TV Presenter

Angie's No Bake Kitty Cat Cookies

For all people who find baking hard or find it hard to find the time to bake.

INGREDIENTS

● 1 packet rich tea biscuits

● 1 packet ready roll fondant icing (white)

● 1 packet in pink

● Small sweets, jelly tots or sprinkled chocolate buttons

● Writing icing tubes (black and red)

● 1 scone cutter slightly smaller than the biscuit.

METHOD

1. Depending on how many cookies you need, to begin with:

2. Roll out white icing and cut out circles, triangles for ears.

3. Roll out pink icing and make tiny triangles to make kitty's bow.

4. Now build the cookies.

5. Slightly dampen fondant circles and place on top of biscuit.

6. Do the same with the ears. Rub the join using a little pressure to hide it.

7. Now the same with pink triangles, place them on cookie to create a bow shape.

8. Squeeze a little writing icing onto sweet and place in the centre of the bow.

9. Now draw on the eyes, whiskers, and a red nose.

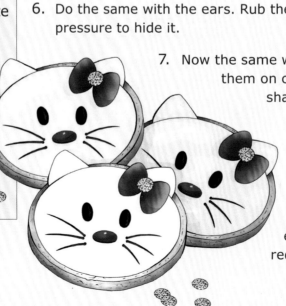

TOM KERRIDGE

Chef Patron, Hand and Flowers, Marlow, Buckinghamshire

Chocolate and Walnut Cookies

INGREDIENTS

THIS WILL MAKE APPROXIMATELY 30–40 COOKIES

- 230g butter
- 365g dark brown sugar
- ½ tbsp salt
- 340g plain flour
- 185g walnuts
- 360g dark chocolate

METHOD

1. Chop walnuts and chocolate.

2. Beat butter, salt and sugar together.

3. Add flour then the chopped nuts and chocolate.

4. Divide the mix into three and roll in cling film to make a sausage shape and set in fridge for a minimum of 3 hours.

5. Once set slice ¼ in thick and bake in the oven at 170°C/340°F/Gas 4 for 8–9 minutes.

 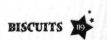

AIMEE WILLMOTT

British Olympic Swimmer,
Team GB 2012

Medley Flapjacks

These flapjacks are one of my favourite snacks to have after training. They're full of goodness, and most importantly easy to make. I like to add that little bit of chocolate to give myself a treat, but with or without these are definitely one to try.

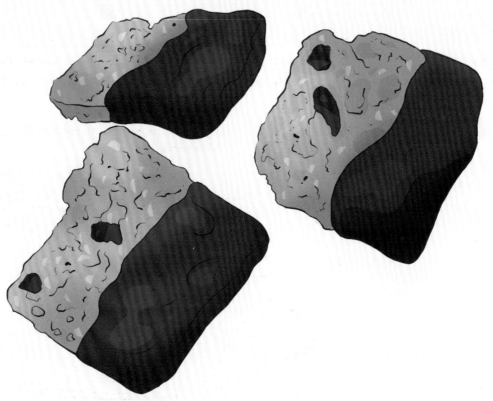

~ INGREDIENTS ~

- 50g walnuts
- 30g dried apricots
- 30g cranberries
- 30g pumpkin seeds
- 4 dried figs
- 100g porridge oats
- 100g rolled oats
- 1 tbsp ground almonds
- 50g butter
- 100g golden syrup
- 100g golden caster sugar
- 100g milk/dark/white chocolate (your choice but I prefer milk chocolate)

~ METHOD ~

1. Preheat the oven to 180C/350F/Gas 4.

2. Put walnuts and pumpkin seeds into a food processor and blitz together but not for long.

3. Cut apricots, cranberries and figs into nice sizable chunks.

4. Put all ingredients in a mixing bowl and add ground almonds.

5. In a pan melt the butter, caster sugar and golden syrup slowly.

6. Once melted add the porridge and rolled oats and rest of dry ingredients.

7. Spread mixture evenly in an oven tray and bake for 25 minutes.

8. When the flapjacks are baked cut into squares and allow to cool.

9. If you wish, melt the chocolate in a bowl over a pan of hot water, dip the flapjacks into the chocolate and chill for about 20 minutes.

10. These taste just as nice without the chocolate.

ED SHAERF

Chef Patron One Blenheim Terrace,
St John's Wood, London

Salted Caramel
Millionaires Shortbread

INGREDIENTS

- 250g plain flour
- 75g caster sugar
- 275g butter, softened
- 100g muscovado sugar
- 800g condensed milk
- 200g milk chocolate
- 1tsp salt

METHOD

1. Pre-heat the oven to 180°C/350°F/Gas 4. Lightly grease a 13x9in/33x23cm Swiss roll tin.

2. To make the shortbread, mix the flour and caster sugar in a bowl. Rub in 175g/6oz butter until mixture resembles breadcrumbs. Knead the mixture together until it forms a dough, then press into the base of the prepared tin. Prick the shortbread lightly and bake in the pre-heated oven for about 18–20 minutes or until very lightly browned. Cool in the tin.

3. To make the caramel, put 100g/3½ oz butter, the muscovado sugar and the condensed milk into a pan and heat gently until the sugar has dissolved. Bring to the boil, stirring all the time, then reduce the heat and simmer very gently, stirring continuously, until the mixture has thickened slightly (about 5 minutes). Add the salt and pour over the shortbread and leave to cool.

4. For the top, melt the chocolate slowly in a bowl over a pan of hot water. Pour over the cold caramel and leave to set. Cut into squares or bars.

ANTONIO CARLUCCIO

Chef/Restaurateur

Polenta Biscuits
Biscotti di Meliga

~ METHOD ~

1. Pre-heat the oven to 190ºC/375ºF/Gas 5.

2. Combine the polenta with the flour and salt then add the butter, cut up into small pieces, and the lemon zest.

3. Mix together to a soft breadcrumb consistency using your finger tips.

4. Beat the eggs and sugar together and then mix into the flour and butter to obtain a soft sticky dough.

5. Butter a large flat baking tin.

6. Using a piping bag with a large nozzle, 1cm (½ in) in diameter, squeeze out 'S' shapes, circles and dots. Don't put them too close to each other as they will spread a little when cooking.

7. Bake in the preheated oven for 15 minutes. The biscuit should be a wonderful gold colour with a darker brown rim. They are very crumbly and delicious.

Copyright©2002 Antonio Carluccio

INGREDIENTS

MAKES 30-40 BISCUITS

- 300g maize flour (polenta, instant or quick cook)

- 110g plain flour

- Pinch of salt

- 200g unsalted butter, plus extra for greasing

- Finely grated zest of ½ lemon

- 2 medium eggs, plus 2 egg yolks

- 300g granulated sugar

BRYN WILLIAMS

Bryn Williams is Chef Proprietor of Odette's Restaurant & Bar in Primrose Hill, London.

Shortbread

INGREDIENTS

MAKES 12–14 GOOD-SIZED FINGERS

- 250g plain flour, plus extra for dusting

- Pinch of salt

- 220g butter, slightly softened

- 100g caster sugar, plus extra for sprinkling

- 1 egg yolk

~ METHOD ~

1. Sift the flour and salt into a bowl. Make a well in the middle of the flour with your hands. Place the butter and sugar in the centre of the well and, using your fingertips, start to bring the flour into the well, rubbing it into the butter and sugar until all the flour has been incorporated.

2. Add the egg yolk. Then, using your hands again, bring the dough together into a ball, wrap it in cling-film and place in the fridge for 2 hours.

3. Pre-heat the oven to 180ºC/350ºF/Gas 4.

4. On a well-floured surface, roll out the dough to a thickness of 5mm. Then, with a sharp knife, cut it into fingers, each about 2cm wide and 8cm long.

5. Place the fingers on the prepared baking tray, sprinkle with a little extra sugar and bake for 12–15 minutes, or until a pale golden colour. Remove from the oven and leave to cool a little on the baking tray before transferring the fingers to a wire rack to cool completely.

www.odettesprimrosehill.com

CHOCOLATE

Cookery Writer/TV Chef/Judge on BBC's The Great British Bake Off

Very Best Chocolate Fudge Cake

"This will become your favourite chocolate cake recipe – it is the best! It is speedy to make and the easy filling doubles as an icing. The cake is moist and has as 'grown-up' chocolate flavour."

INGREDIENTS

- 50g sifted cocoa powder
- 6 tbsp boiling water

- 3 large eggs
- 50ml/2fl oz milk

- 175g self-raising flour
- 1 rounded tsp baking powder
- 100g softened butter
- 275g caster sugar

ICING AND FILLING

- 3 tbsp apricot jam
- 150g plain chocolate (39% cocoa solids)
- 150ml/¼ pint double cream

1. Preheat the oven to 180°C/350°F/Fan 160°C/325°F/Gas 4.

2. Grease two 20cm (8in) deep sandwich tins then line the base of each with baking parchment.

3. Blend the cocoa and boiling water in a large bowl then add the remaining cake ingredients and beat until the mixture has become a smooth, thickish batter. Divide the cake mix equally between the prepared tins and level the surface.

4. Bake in the pre-heated oven for about 25-30 minutes or until well risen and the tops of the cakes spring back when lightly pressed with a finger. Leave to cool in the tins for a few minutes then turn out, peel off the parchment and finish cooling on a wire rack.

5. To make the icing, warm the apricot jam in a very small pan, then spread a little over the base of one cake and the top of the other. Break the chocolate into pieces and gently heat with the cream in a heatproof bowl set over a pan of simmering water for about 10 minutes or just until the chocolate has melted, stirring occasionally.

6. Remove the bowl from the heat and stir the chocolate mixture to make sure it has completely melted. Leave to cool until it is on the point of setting then spread on top of the apricot on both cakes. Sandwich the cakes together and use a small palette knife to smooth the icing on the top. Keep in a cool place until ready to serve.

MARY'S TOP TIP

The cake can be frozen (iced or un-iced) for up to 1 month. Store in a round freezer-proof container about 2.5cm (1in) bigger than the diameter of the cake. Sit the cake on the inside of the lid and place the container over the top. Seal, label and freeze. If the cake is frozen iced, the icing will not be quite as shiny once thawed. To defrost, release the lid but leave in position and thaw for 4 hours at room temperature.

MARTINE McCUTCHEON

Actress

Mum's Choccie Cake

~ INGREDIENTS ~

TAKES 45 MINUTES TO PREPARE AND COOK.

FOR THE CAKE

- 175g dark chocolate
- 200g unsalted butter
- 200g self-raising flour
- 300g brown sugar
- 2 tbsp cocoa
- 1 tsp baking powder
- 4 large eggs
- 2 tbsp condensed milk

FOR THE FILLING

- 40g icing sugar
- 1 tbsp cocoa powder
- 30g unsalted butter

TO DECORATE

- Large slab of chocolate
- Mini Flakes

~ METHOD ~

1. Pre-heat oven to 350°F/180°C/Gas 4. Grease 2x20cm baking cake tins and line with greaseproof paper.

2. Place a bowl over a boiling saucepan of water and melt the butter and sugar.

3. Sift the flour, cocoa and baking powder into a mixing bowl.

4. Mix in the eggs and condensed milk, add the melted butter and sugar then stir until smooth and soft.

5. Split the mixture between the two baking tins and bake in the oven for about 30-40 minutes.

6. To make the filling, mix the icing sugar, butter and cocoa together until smooth. Leave in the fridge until needed.

7. To make the topping, melt the chocolate in a bowl over hot water until smooth.

8. When the cakes have cooled, take one sponge and smooth the butter icing over it then nestle the second sponge on top.

9. Drizzle the melted chocolate all over the cake and top with the mini flakes.

JANE ASHER

Actress/Author/Baker

American Brownies

A brownie is to a slice of chocolate cake as rock and roll is to jazz: just as satisfying in its own way but with a more accessible, younger feel that, at the right time, hits the spot perfectly. And Brownies were invented – just as rock and roll was – in the US, and this simple but wonderfully dense and chewy recipe reminds me of the brownies I used to eat warm with vanilla ice cream in Joe Allen's restaurant in New York.

A recipe from Jane Asher from her book, Beautiful Baking, published by Simon & Schuster

MAKES 10 GENEROUS BROWNIES

- 200ml vegetable oil
- 150g golden granulated sugar
- 100g dark brown soft sugar
- 2 tsps vanilla extract
- 3 medium eggs
- 60g cocoa powder
- 100g self raising flour
- ¼ tsp salt
- ¼ tsp sodium bicarbonate
- 100g chopped hazelnuts or walnuts (optional)

~◦ METHOD ◦~

1. Pre-heat the oven to 180°C (165°C fan assisted, 350°F, gas mark 4). Prepare an 20cm x 25cm/8" x 10" (or 23cm/9" square) baking tray by brushing the bottom and sides with a little vegetable oil and slipping a re-usable silicone liner (or a piece of baking parchment) of the right size in the bottom.

2. Put all the ingredients into a large mixing bowl and beat well together.

3. Spoon the mixture into the prepared tin and bake for 25-30 minutes, depending on how chewy you like your brownies (I like to take them out when the centre is just set, but not yet firm)

4. Let the brownies cool in the tin (unless you want to eat them warm), then turn out and then decorate.

DECORATING IDEAS

You can simply serve the brownies sprinkled with a little sieved icing sugar, or cover them with chocolate butter icing or chocolate frosting, then decorate with nuts or chocolate drops. For very special occasions, they look fantastic with a few gold dragees or edible glitter on top. Serve with a dollop of crème fraiche, whipped cream or ice cream.

JOANNE WHEATLEY

Winner of BBC's The Great British Bake Off 2011

Chocolate Orange Cake

~ INGREDIENTS ~

- 280g self-raising flour
- 280g margarine
- 280g caster sugar
- 5 eggs
- 55g cocoa

- 1 tsp vanilla paste
- Fillings:
- 150ml/5fl oz double cream whipped with orange zest (save a little for topping)

- 3 large tablespoons chocolate nutella spread
- Juice and zest of a large orange
- Icing sugar

~ METHOD ~

1. Preheat oven to 170°C/325°F/Gas 3.

2. Mix all of the ingredients together in a freestanding mixer (I use my Kitchen Aid) or with handheld whisk until nice and fluffy.

3. Spoon into 2 prepared tins (18cm/7in sandwich).

4. Cook for about 25/30 minutes depending on oven (could be as long as 35 minutes).

5. Leave to cool on wire racks.

6. Sandwich together with fillings:

7. Spread chocolate spread onto one side of the cake.

8. Mix juice and icing sugar to make a runny icing, spread onto the other inside of the cake.

9. Pipe or spoon double cream onto either cake then sandwich them together.

10. If you wish to, pipe rosettes onto the top and finish it off with orange zest and chocolate shavings.

DENISE VAN OUTEN

Actress/Singer/TV presenter

Chocolate Truffle Fudge Cake

This is delicious and so easy as it doesn't even need an oven. All the work is in the measuring. Also good as it stays fresh for a good few days in an air-tight tin.

INGREDIENTS

- 250g butter
- 55g caster sugar
- 2 tbsp golden syrup
- 2 tbsp milk
- 2 tbsp drinking chocolate
- 1 tbsp cocoa
- 500g packet of digestives – crushed or blitzed in food processor
- 75g of chocolate cake crumbs
- Nip of rum or whisky
- 60g glace cherries
- 75g raisins
- 250g dark chocolate

METHOD

1. Melt butter, sugar, milk and golden syrup over gentle heat in a large saucepan.

2. Once the sugar has dissolved add cocoa, drinking chocolate and half of the biscuits.

3. Mix well and then add all the remaining ingredients, except for the chocolate.

4. Press the mixture into a 20cm/8in square tin.

5. Melt the dark chocolate over a pan of boiling water.

6. Once done, spread it over the biscuit base and leave to set.

7. This should make 30 small bars. Delicious!

 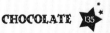

CHEMMY ALCOTT

Olympic Skier and contestant on
Dancing on Ice 2011

Chocolate Chilli Cake

~ INGREDIENTS ~

- 250ml/9fl oz semi-skimmed milk

- 100g dark chocolate (70% cocoa) broken up

- ¼ tsp ground ginger

- ¼ tsp Tabasco sauce

- 250g plain flour + 1 tbsp cocoa powder

- 2 tsp baking powder

- ½ tsp bicarbonate of soda

- 150g unsalted butter, softened

- 300g light brown muscovado sugar

- 1 tbsp black treacle

- 3 large free-range eggs

- Extra cocoa powder or icing sugar for dusting

METHOD

1. Pre-heat oven to 180°C/350°F/Gas 4.

2. Grease 900g/2lb loaf tin and line with baking paper or 2x450g/1lb tins.

3. Heat milk in small pan until hot, but not boiling.

4. Remove from heat and add chocolate, ginger and Tabasco, stirring gently until melted and smooth. Leave to cool.

5. Meanwhile sieve the flour, cocoa powder, baking powder and bicarbonate of soda in a bowl. Put to one side.

6. Put soft butter in a mixing bowl and use a mixer until it is creamy.

7. Make sure the sugar is lump-free and beat it into the butter, followed by the treacle. Continue to beat thoroughly for about 5 minutes or until the mixture looks paler and fluffy.

8. Beat the eggs with a fork and then gradually add to the mixture, beating well.

9. Using a large metal spoon, stir in the flour in 3 batches, alternating with the cold chocolate milk. When combined pour into the tin(s), spreading evenly.

10. Bake for 55–60 minutes (for the smaller tins, 40–50 minutes), or until firm and a skewer inserted into the centre comes out clean. Leave to cool in the tin for 5 minutes and don't worry if the cake shrinks slightly.

11. Put on a wire rack and cool completely.

12. Dust with cocoa powder or icing sugar.

13. Enjoy with a nice strong, frothy coffee.

Photograph: David
Fisher/Rex Features

FEARNE COTTON

Radio/TV Presenter

Chocolate Cupcakes with a Buttercream Topping

INGREDIENTS

FOR THE CUPCAKES

- 150g butter
- 150g caster sugar
- 175g self-raising flour
- 25g cocoa powder

- 3 eggs

FOR THE BUTTERCREAM TOPPING

- 250g butter
- 500g icing sugar (sifted)

- 2 drops of vanilla extract
- 2 tsp milk
- 12 raspberries
- Chocolate flakes (or chocolate chips)

METHOD

FOR THE CUPCAKES

1. Pre-heat the oven to 180ºC/350ºF/Gas 4.

2. Lay out 12 cupcake cases on a baking tray/muffin tin.

3. Beat the eggs with a fork in a separate bowl.

4. Using an electric mixer, mix the butter, sugar, flour and cocoa powder in a bowl adding the beaten eggs slowly into the bowl as you are mixing.

5. Using a large spoon place equal amounts of mixture into the 12 cupcake cases.

6. Put the cupcakes into the oven (near the top) and bake for 15–20 minutes. Check on them after 15 minutes, they should be firm to touch (or you can test by popping a skewer into the middle of the cupcake & it should come out clean), if not leave them in for a further 5 minutes.

7. Remove from the oven & leave to cool. Once cooled add the buttercream!

FOR THE BUTTERCREAM TOPPING

1. Place the butter into a bowl and stir in the icing sugar and vanilla extract using a wooden spoon then whisk (again using an electric mixer) until fluffy and lighter in colour. Add 2 tsp of milk and whisk again. If the mixture is still too stiff add a little more milk.

2. Put the buttercream mixture into a piping bag with a large star nozzle and then squeeze plenty of buttercream onto each cupcake (make sure the cupcakes are cool first).

3. Sprinkle chocolate flakes or chocolate chips over the top of the buttercream, finally add a raspberry to the top.

ERIC LANLARD

Chef

Cream Cheese Brownies

This takes the best of a rich, traditional brownie, but gives it a twist: the soft cream cheese adds a soft touch as well as a fresh sour-zesty taste.

INGREDIENTS

MAKES 12 BROWNIES

Preparation time: 30 minutes. Cooking time: 30 minutes

FOR THE CAKE

- 150g unsalted butter, plus extra for greasing
- 200g dark chocolate, broken into pieces
- 100ml/3½ fl oz freshly made strong espresso
- 250g caster sugar
- 1 tsp vanilla extract
- Pinch of salt
- 3 eggs
- 100g plain flour

FOR THE MARBLING MIXTURE

- 150g cream cheese
- 60g caster sugar
- 1 egg, beaten
- 1 tsp vanilla extract

METHOD

1. Preheat the oven to 180°C (Fan 160°C)/350°F/Gas 4.

2. Grease a 20cm /8in square tin with extra butter, and line it with baking paper.

3. Melt the butter and the chocolate in a large heatproof bowl over a pan of gently simmering water, stirring occasionally (the bowl should not touch the water).

4. Remove the bowl from the heat and cool slightly.

5. Stir the sugar, vanilla and salt into the butter-chocolate mixture, then whisk in the eggs, using a wooden spoon or electric hand whisk, and beat until smooth.

6. Stir in the coffee, then sift in the flour and carry on beating until glossy. Set aside.

7. For the marbling mixture, in a bowl beat the cream cheese until smooth, then stir in the sugar, egg and vanilla.

8. Spoon the dark mixture into the prepared tin first, then add the cheese marbling mixture and use a knife to cut through to create a marbled effect.

9. Bake in the preheated oven for 30 minutes.

10. You may need to cover the tin with foil for the last 10 minutes of cooking.

11. Allow to cool in the tin, then cut into squares.

Taken from Home Bake by Eric Lanlard, published by Mitchell Beazley

LAUREN GOODGER

Reality TV Star from
The Only Way Is Essex (TOWIE)

Rocky Road

INGREDIENTS

- 100g butter, roughly chopped

- 300g dark chocolate, broken into squares

- 3 tbsp golden syrup

- 140g rich tea biscuits, roughly crushed

- 12 pink marshmallows, quartered using scissors

- 2 x 55g of either Maltesers (my favourite), Milky Way or Crunchie

~ METHOD ~

1. Gently melt the butter, chocolate and syrup in a large pan over a low heat, stirring frequently until smooth, then cool for about 15 minutes.

2. Stir the crushed biscuits and sweets into the pan until well mixed, pour into a 17cm/6½in square tin lined with non-stick baking paper and spread the mixture to roughly level it.

3. Chill until hard and then take out of tin and remove paper.

4. Cut into fingers.

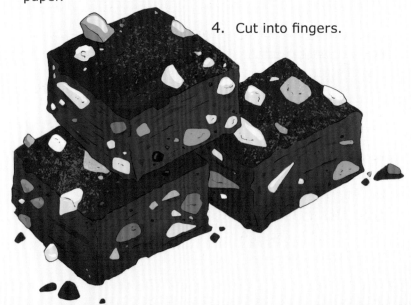

FRANCESCO MAZZEI

Chef-Patron, L'Anima, London

Chocolate Cake

❧ INGREDIENTS ❧

- 300g Valrhona guanaja chocolate (70%)
- 120g butter
- 4 egg yolks
- 6 egg whites

- 300g sugar
- Few drops lemon juice

MASCARPONE CREAM FILLING

- 50g egg yolk

- 50g sugar
- 500g mascarpone cheese

MIXED BERRIES

- 50g blueberries

- 50g raspberries
- 50g blackberries
- 50g redcurrants
- 2 tbsp sugar
- 1 lemon
- 10 mint leaves

❧ METHOD ❧

1. Melt the chocolate and butter together. Grease a cake tin with butter.

2. Once melted add the egg yolks and whipped egg whites to the sugar and lemon juice. Fold the meringue into the chocolate and bake it at 170°C/325°F/Gas 3 for 22–25 minutes.

MASCARPONE CREAM FILLING

1. Whip the egg yolk with sugar. Once it turns white add mascarpone cheese. Whisk it and allow to set in the container in the fridge.

MIXED BERRIES

1. Wash all berries and place in a bowl, add sugar, lemon juice from squeezed lemon and julienne from mint leaves. Mix it.

2. Cut a slice of chocolate cake, dust with cocoa powder. Put a spoon of mascarpone cream and spoon of mixed berries on the side.

TRISTAN WELCH

Food Network UK Chef

Chocolate and Hazelnut Brownie, Cheat's Raspberry Ripple Sorbet

INGREDIENTS

SERVES 6-8

- 300g whole hazelnuts

- 275g 70% chocolate

- 225g butter

- 400g caster sugar

- 1 tsp vanilla essence

- Pinch of salt

- 5 eggs

- 200g plain flour

- 27cm/10¾ in diameter cake tin (brushed with butter and then dusted in flour)

SORBET

- 80g icing sugar

- 2 x packets frozen raspberries

- 4 tbsp double cream

METHOD

1. Pre-heat the oven to 150°C/300°F/ Gas 2.

2. Take a microwave proof bowl, place the chocolate, butter, caster sugar, vanilla and salt in and melt it all together in a microwave set to medium, should take no longer than 2–3 minutes depending on your microwave.

3. Once all is melted, crack the eggs in one by one mixing each one into the chocolate before cracking the next.

4. Fold in the flour and then walnuts, pour into the cake tin.

5. Bake at 150°C/300°F/Gas 2 for 25 minutes, then allow the brownie to cool to room temperature before serving.

TO MAKE THE SORBET

1. Take the frozen raspberries and place them in a food processor with the icing sugar, blend them while still very frozen.

2. As soon as the raspberries are smooth, turn off the food processor, add the cream then blend 2–3 times using the pulse button to get the ripple effect.

3. Serve immediately or you can keep in your freezer until you would like to serve it.

EMMA BUNTON

Former Spice Girl,
TV and Radio Presenter

Delicious Squidgy
Chocolate Cake!

~ INGREDIENTS ~

- 150g unsalted butter, plus more for greasing

- 200g dark chocolate drops, minimum 70% cocoa solids

- 150g caster sugar

- 100g ground almonds

- 5 eggs, separated

CHOCOLATE BUTTERCREAM

- 175g butter, softened

- 125g cocoa powder

- 650g icing sugar

- 150ml/5fl oz. milk

- 1 tsp vanilla extract

~ METHOD ~

1. Preheat the oven to 180°C/350°F/Gas Mark 4.

2. Grease a deep 20cm round cake tin with butter and sprinkle lightly with flour or, preferably, use a non-stick liner.

3. Put the butter, chocolate drops and sugar into a heatproof bowl and melt together, either in a microwave oven or in a bowl over a pan of hot (not boiling) water. Stir well until it becomes smooth. Allow to cool a little, then stir in the ground almonds.

4. Stir the egg yolks into the yummy chocolate mixture.

5. In a large bowl, whisk the egg whites until stiff, then stir gently into the chocolate.

6. Turn the mixture into the cake tin and bake for 35-45 minutes, depending on how squidgy you like it.

7. Let it cool a little, then remove from the tin and cool completely on a rack.

8. Then add lashings of chocolate buttercream on top of the cake. EAT!!

LEONA LEWIS

Singer and winner of
The X Factor 2006

Chocolate Cupcakes with Mint Choc Chip Icing

INGREDIENTS

- 150g soft butter
- 150g caster sugar
- 175g self-raising flour
- 3 eggs
- 2 tbsp cocoa
- 1 tsp vanilla extract

MINT CHOC-CHIP ICING

- 140g unsalted or slightly salted soft butter
- 250g sifted icing sugar

- 2–3 tsp peppermint essence (adjust to taste)
- 75g dark chocolate finely chopped or whizzed in a food processor
- Green food colouring

METHOD

1. Pre-heat oven to 180°C/350°F/Gas 4.

2. Line a cupcake tin with 12 papers.

3. Beat eggs lightly in a cup.

4. Cream butter and sugar in a large bowl.

5. Place all the rest of the ingredients into the bowl with the creamed butter and sugar.

6. Beat with an electric mixer for about 2 minutes until mixture is light and creamy.

7. Bake for about 18–20 minutes until risen and firm to touch.

8. Allow to cool for a few minutes and then transfer to a wire rack. Allow to cool before icing.

9. Beat butter in large mixing bowl with electric mixer until fluffy and smooth.

10. Add about one cup of sifted icing sugar to butter and beat until combined. Continue one cup at a time until all of the sugar is incorporated.

11. Add peppermint essence to taste and then the green food colouring. Gradually add chocolate chip pieces, and ice cakes.

Photograph: Gareth Morgans

Food stylist/Writer/TV Chef

Double Chocolate and Pecan Brownies

There are numerous recipes for chocolate brownies, but I think these tick all the boxes – deliciously rich and gooey with a crisp top, and packed full of cheeky little white chocolate and pecan nut chunks. They're impossible to resist.

~ INGREDIENTS ~

TAKES ABOUT 25 MINUTES TO BAKE

MAKES 12 GOOD-SIZED BROWNIES

- 200g unsalted butter
- 200g dark chocolate

(70% cocoa solids), chopped

- 3 eggs
- 300g granulated sugar
- 2 tsp vanilla extract

- 125g plain flour
- Pinch of salt
- 150g white chocolate chunks
- 150g pecan nuts, roughly chopped

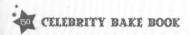

~ METHOD ~

1. Preheat the oven to 180°C/350°F/Fan 160°C/Gas 4.

2. Grease and line an approximately 20x30cm rectangular baking tin, 3–4cm deep, with greaseproof or parchment paper.

3. Melt the butter and dark chocolate either in a bowl over a pan of simmering water or gently in the microwave.

4. With an electric hand whisk, beat together the eggs, sugar and vanilla extract until they are lovely and thick and creamy. Mix in the melted chocolate and butter. Finally stir in the flour, salt, white chocolate chunks and chopped pecans.

5. Pour into the baking tin and cook for about 25 minutes until the top is cracking and the centre is just set. Leave to cool in the tin for about 20 minutes before cutting into squares.

6. Serve warm or, if you can resist leaving them, cold.

PS...

1. To serve the brownies as a dessert, whip up this delicious orange mascarpone cream to serve with them. Beat together 200g mascarpone, 50g sifted icing sugar and the finely grated zest of 1 small orange until you have a smooth, creamy mixture. If it seems too thick, just beat in some milk to loosen. Serve a big spoonful on top of the warm brownies so it melts over them.

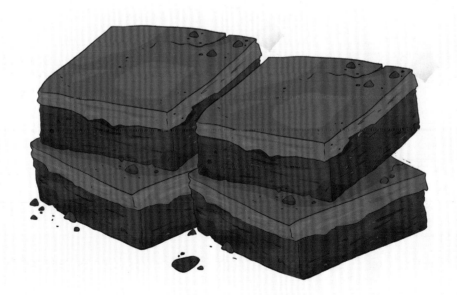

GEMMA COLLINS

Reality TV Star from
The Only Way Is Essex (TOWIE)

I Can't Believe You Made That Cake

(Created by Lorraine Pascale)

~ INGREDIENTS ~

- Vegetable oil or oil spray
- 200g butter, softened
- 200g caster sugar
- 4 free-range eggs
- 140g plain flour
- 60g cocoa powder
- Pinch of salt
- 2 tsp baking powder

- 400g plain, milk, or white chocolate cigarillos (about 75-80 in total)

FOR THE BUTTERCREAM

- 250g butter, softened
- 500g icing sugar
- 100g good dark chocolate (at least 70% cocoa solids), melted

and slightly cooled

FOR THE DECORATION

- Fresh flowers, for a Christening cake
- Strawberries or raspberries, for the girls
- Figs, quartered, for the boys

This recipe is reprinted by permission of HarperCollins Publishers Ltd

From BAKING MADE EASY by LORRAINE PASCALE

~❧ METHOD ❧~

1. Preheat the oven to 180ºC/350ºF/Gas 4 and line a 20cm/8in round deep cake tin with baking paper and brush or spray with oil.

2. Cream together the butter and sugar in a large bowl until they begin to go pale. Add half of the eggs and half of the flour and mix well. Add the rest of the eggs, flour, cocoa powder, salt and baking powder and beat for a minute or two until the mixture is uniform. Dollop into the prepared tin and bake in the oven for about 30-40 minutes, or until a skewer inserted in the middle comes out clean. Leave to cool in the tin.

3. Meanwhile, make the buttercream: put the butter and icing sugar in a bowl and whisk together until the mixture goes fluffy. Add the cooled, melted chocolate and whisk for a further two minutes.

4. Once the cake is completely cool, remove it from the tin. Carefully cut the top flat with a large serrated knife.

(Eat this bit as a chef's perk!)

5. Turn the cake upside down on a 20cm/8in cake board so that the bottom now becomes a nice flat top. Split the cake horizontally and sandwich the top and bottom together with a 1cm/½in layer of buttercream.

6. Spread half of the remaining buttercream all over the top and sides of the cake, making it as smooth as possible. Put it in the fridge to set before doing another layer – this makes it much easier to get neat squared-off edges.

7. Gently push the cigarillos vertically onto the sides of the cake, positioning them as straight as possible and making sure they touch the bottom.

8. The next step is up to you – I can't tell you the wide-eyed looks you'll get when you walk into a room holding this finished cake.

9. Serve with a self-satisfied grin.

TOM KITCHIN

Chef Patron, The Kitchin, Edinburgh

Chocolate Tart

~INGREDIENTS~

SERVES 6-8

SWEET PASTRY

- 500g plain flour
- 100g icing sugar
- 350g cold unsalted butter, cut into cubes

- 1 egg

CHOCOLATE FILLING

- 450g dark chocolate
- 300g butter
- 1 shot Grand Marnier

- 6 whole eggs
- 5 egg yolks
- 60g caster sugar
- Vanilla
- Icing sugar for serving

~METHOD~

TO MAKE THE PASTRY

1. Sift the flour and sugar together. Pulse with the butter in the food processor until the mixture resembles breadcrumbs. Mix in the egg and knead gently until the dough clings together. Flatten to a round, wrap in clingfilm and chill in the fridge for 15 minutes.

2. Pre-heat the oven to 200ºC/400ºF/Gas 6. Roll out the pastry to a thickness of about 4mm and line in a 23cm pie tin or fluted flan case. Trim the edges and add some parchment paper and 3 cups of baking beans.

3. Bake in the pre-heated oven for 10 minutes, then remove the beans and paper and cook for another 10-12 minutes or until golden.

4. While the pastry is still warm brush the inside with beaten egg. This helps to seal the pastry from the tart filling, ensuring a crispy base.

TO MAKE THE CHOCOLATE FILLING

1. Place chocolate, butter and Grand Marnier in a bowl. Cover tightly with cling-film and place the bowl over a pan of simmering water.

2. Allow the chocolate and butter to melt gently until there are no lumps left. Leave to cool.

3. Preheat the oven to 150ºC/300ºF/ Gas 2. Whisk together the whole eggs, egg yolks, caster sugar and vanilla until tripled in volume. Fold this slowly into the warm chocolate mixture until completely incorporated.

4. Pour the chocolate filling into the cooked tart shell and bake for 20–25 minutes. Leave to set at room temperature for 15 minutes, then put the tart into the fridge for at least an hour to finish setting.

BARRY MCGUIGAN

Commentator and Boxing column writer for the Daily Mirror/ Former Boxing Champion

The Black Stuff

Barry's version of 'The Black Stuff!'. It is chocolate but it has twist as it has meringue on top and is supposed to look like a pint of Guinness! Essentially it's an alcohol-free indulgence!

INGREDIENTS

All eggs are large, and free range where possible.

Bring all ingredients to room temperature before beginning.

FOR THE CAKE BASE:

- 240g quality dark chocolate

- 115g good Irish butter

- 5 eggs

- 240g caster sugar

- 20g cocoa powder

FOR THE MERINGUE TOPPING:

- 8 large egg whites

- ¼ tsp cream of tartar

- 315g caster sugar

～ METHOD ～

FOR THE CAKE BASE:

1. Pre-heat oven to 180°C/350°F/Gas 4. Grease a 9in/23cm spring-form tin, place on a foil-lined baking tray, and set aside.

2. Melt the chocolate and butter in a pyrex bowl over a pan of simmering water until melted, stirring often.

3. Meanwhile, whisk the eggs and sugar with an electric mixer until it falls in thick ribbons from the whisk. This should take approximately 2 minutes. You can do this by hand but it will take much longer and you need to be prepared to hurt!

4. Add the cocoa powder and mix on a low speed until combined. Add the melted chocolate mix and fold into the cocoa egg mixture gently until combined, taking care to keep the air in the mix.

5. Pour this batter into your prepared cake tin, and bake for 12 minutes. Rotate the tray and bake for another 8–10 minutes, or until the surface of cake is just firm to the touch but still has a little bit of a wobble in the middle. Place on a cooling rack and allow to come to room temperature while you get on with the meringue topping.

FOR THE MERINGUE TOPPING:

1. Pre-heat oven to 190°C/375°F/Gas 5.

2. Place the egg whites and cream of tartar in a bowl. Start whipping the egg whites/tartar mix until frothy. Now, slowly, start adding in the sugar little by little, until the meringue is thick and glossy and stiff peaks form.

3. Pile the meringue onto the cooled cake. Spread it to within an inch of the outer edge of the cooled cake base, try to keep this smooth, but feel free to add in a traditional shamrock for effect, depending on how creative you're feeling.

4. Bake in your preheated oven for 12–15 minutes, until meringue is lightly browned. You can serve immediately, but it's just as good cold.

LUCIANA BERGER MP

Shadow Minister for
Energy and Climate Change

Milk Chocolate Cake

~ METHOD ~

1. Heat oven to 180ºC/350ºF/Gas Mark 4. Grease 2 x 20.5 cm (8 inch) tins, not loose-bottomed as the mixture would run out.

2. Mix flour, sugar, salt and cocoa.

3. Rub in margarine. Beat eggs with milk.

4. Stir egg mixture, essence and liquids into the dry ingredients and beat well.

5. Place mixture in prepared tins and bake for about 30-35 minutes.

6. When cold sandwich with melted Mars Bar and top with Milk Chocolate Icing.

INGREDIENTS

- 200g Be-Ro self raising flour

- 225g caster sugar

- 1½ tsp salt

- 25g cocoa powder, sieved

- 100g margarine

- 2 medium eggs

- 5 tbsp evaporated milk

- 5 tbsp water

- Few drops vanilla essence

EFFIE WOODS

Actress

Chocolate Orange Muffins

~ METHOD ~

1. Pre-heat oven to 180°C/350°F/Gas 4.

2. Line a muffin tin with 12 muffin cases – the tulip ones work best but regular ones are ok.

3. In one bowl sift together the flour, salt, baking powder and sugar.

4. In another bowl or jug, mix together the egg, milk, yogurt, melted butter and orange zest. Put chocolate chunks in 1 tbsp of flour to coat the pieces – this helps to stop them sinking to the bottom of your muffin.

5. Mix wet ingredients into dry ingredients and stir together lightly until just combined. Fold in chocolate chunks. The mixture will be quite thick and lumpy but don't be tempted to over-mix!

6. Spoon into your muffin cases. Bake for approximately 20 minutes, until the tops are golden and spring back when gently prodded. Cool on a wire rack. Enjoy zingy, chocolatey goodness!

INGREDIENTS

MAKES 10-12

- 250g plain flour
- 3 tsp baking powder
- ½ tsp salt
- 100g caster sugar
- 1 egg, beaten
- 100ml/3½fl oz milk
- 100g plain yoghurt
- 60g melted butter
- Zest of 2 large oranges
- 100g dark chocolate, chopped into chunks

TANIA BRYER

TV Presenter

Chocolate Brownies

INGREDIENTS

- 90g plain chocolate

- 150g unsalted butter and extra for greasing the tin

- 125g plain flour

- 15g cocoa powder

- 3 eggs

- 300g soft light brown sugar

- Pinch of salt

- 1 tsp vanilla extract

- ½ tsp baking powder

- 100g chopped pecan nuts (optional)

METHOD

1. Preheat the oven to 180°C/350°F/Gas 4. Grease and line the base of the baking tin with baking paper.

2. Break the chocolate into a bowl and add the butter. Melt the butter and chocolate over a saucepan of boiling water. Stirring occasionally till totally melted.

3. Remove the bowl from the heat and allow to cool slightly. Sieve the flour, cocoa powder, baking powder and salt into a separate bowl.

4. In a third bowl, beat the eggs and then add the sugar and vanilla extract. Stir the ingredients together until they are combined.

5. Fold the melted chocolate into the beaten egg mixture, then fold in the flour mixture and nuts. There should be no visible flour.

6. Spoon the mixture into the tin, smooth the top with a palette knife and bake for about 25 minutes.

7. Allow to cool in the tin before cutting into squares.

Photograph: Simon Songhurst

CLAUDIA WINKLEMAN
TV Presenter

Easy Peasy Chocolate Cake

~ INGREDIENTS ~

- 55g self-raising flour
- 55g ground almonds
- 115g caster sugar
- 115g unsalted butter
- 115g drinking

chocolate
- 3 eggs (large)
- ½ tsp baking powder

TOPPING
- 55g dark chocolate

- 25g butter
- 1 tbsp top of milk or cream
- Icing sugar

~ METHOD ~

1. Pre-heat oven to 170°C/325°F/Gas 3.

2. Cream butter and sugar together in food processor or mixer.

3. Sieve together all dry ingredients.

4. With each egg add one third of dry ingredients to creamed mixture.

5. Grease round 20cm/8in deep cake tin with butter and flour.

6. Bake for about 40–50 minutes until risen and a skewer inserted into the centre comes out clean.

7. Remove from tin after about 5 minutes.

TOPPING

1. Use ¾ of the chocolate and melt in a bain-marie pan (bowl over hot water) with the butter. Remove from heat.

2. Beat gently until smooth and stir in the milk or cream.

3. Add enough icing sugar to make coating consistency (just enough to coat the back of a spoon).

4. Pour onto the cooled cake and grate the remaining chocolate over the top.

STACIE STEWART

Baker/Cook/Owner of the Beehive Bakery

Hot Chocolate and Churros

It's freezing outside, indulge with this evening treat.
Perfect for weekend lazy days too!

INGREDIENTS

SERVES 4

HOT CHOCOLATE

- 100g plain chocolate, with at least 70% cocoa solids, broken up

- 350ml whole milk

FOR THE CHURROS

- Vegetable or sunflower oil, for deep-frying

- 100g plain flour, sieved

- 150ml/5fl oz

whole milk

- 100ml/3½ fl oz water

- 2 eggs, beaten

- 50g caster sugar

- 1 heaped tsp ground cinnamon

~ METHOD ~

1. In a large, deep pan, heat the oil for deep-frying the churros to 190°C or until a piece of bread takes 30 seconds to colour.

2. Bring the milk and 100ml water to the boil in a pan, add the flour and beat with a wooden spoon until smooth. Cool slightly, then gradually beat in enough egg to make a smooth but stiff, glossy mixture. It should drop off the spoon but not be too runny.

3. Spoon this mix into a piping bag with a large star nozzle. If you don't have a star nozzle just snip the end off a piping bag to make a hole around the size of a 10p piece.

4. Holding the nozzle over the hot oil, gently squeeze the piping bag and snip off 6-8 lengths of the mixture with kitchen scissors, they should be around 10cm each.

5. Fry for 4–5 minutes, turning occasionally, until crisp and golden brown. Lift out with a slotted spoon onto a baking tray lined with kitchen paper.

6. Put the chocolate in a heatproof bowl and rest over a pan of simmering water until completely melted. Alternatively melt in a microwave on 30 second bursts, stirring after each interval.

7. Meanwhile, bring the milk to the boil in a small pan. Remove the chocolate from the heat and whisk in a little of the hot milk. Add the rest and whisk until frothy. Pour into hot mugs.

8. Mix the sugar and cinnamon and toss with the churros gently until lightly coated. Serve for dipping into the hot chocolate while curled up on the sofa.

Photograph:
Georgia Glynn Smith ©

PEGGY PORSCHEN

Baker/Cake Designer/Patron of
Peggy Porschen Parlour, London

Chocolate Heaven Cupcakes

INGREDIENTS

MAKES ABOUT 24 CUPCAKES

FOR THE FROSTING

- 140ml whipping cream
- 160g plain chocolate (minimum 53% cocoa solids),
- chopped or in buttons
- 1 tbsp glucose
- 200g full-fat cream cheese
- 200g salted butter, softened
- 450g icing sugar, sifted

FOR THE CAKE MIX

- 125g plain chocolate (minimum 53% cocoa solids),
- chopped or in buttons
- 165ml milk
- 285g light brown sugar
- 105g unsalted butter, softened
- 2 large eggs
- 180g plain flour
- Pinch of salt

- ½ tsp baking powder
- ½ tsp bicarbonate of soda
- 8g cocoa powder

EQUIPMENT

- Two 12-hole muffin trays
- 24 large brown cupcake cases
- Plastic piping bag
- Large star piping nozzle
- 24 pearlised scallop-edged cupcake wrappers

BOUTIQUE BAKING by PEGGY PORSCHEN, published by Quadrille (£20, hardback)

1. Preheat the oven to 160°C/325°F/Gas 3. Prepare the muffin trays by placing the cupcake cases inside the holes.

TO MAKE THE FROSTING

1. Place the cream in a saucepan and bring to a bare simmer. Place the chocolate and glucose into a bowl and pour the hot cream over the top. Whisk together until smooth, shiny and all the chocolate has melted. Once combined, leave to set at room temperature; the Ganache should have the consistency of soft butter.

2. Place the cream cheese into a mixing bowl and beat until smooth and creamy.

3. Place the butter and icing sugar into a separate mixing bowl and cream together until very pale and fluffy.

4. Add the ganache, a little at a time, to the buttercream mixture and mix at medium-high speed until the frosting is combined.

5. Gently stir one-third of the chocolate buttercream into the cream cheese.

6. Slowly whisk the remaining buttercream and add the chocolate cream cheese in two batches. Take care not to overwork the frosting as it can split. Chill until set.

TO MAKE THE CUPCAKES

1. Place the chocolate, milk and half the sugar into a saucepan. Gently bring to the boil whilst stirring.

2. Place the butter and remaining sugar in a mixing bowl and cream together until very pale and fluffy.

3. Beat the eggs lightly in another bowl and slowly stir into the butter mixture.

4. Sift the flour, baking powder, bicarbonate of soda, salt and cocoa powder together and add to the batter in two batches. Slowly mix until just combined.

5. Slowly pour the hot chocolate into the batter and mix. Scrape the bowl with a rubber spatula to make sure the batter is well combined. Transfer the batter to a measuring jug.

6. While still warm, pour the batter into the cupcake cases until two-thirds full.

7. Bake immediately for 12–15 minutes, depending on your oven. The cupcakes are cooked when tops spring back to the touch and the edges have shrunk away from the side. Once cooked, the texture of this sponge is slightly sticky and dense. If you insert a clean knife or wooden skewer into the centre of the sponge, it should come out with a small amount of crumb sticking to it.

8. Once the cupcakes are baked let them rest for a few minutes outside the oven. Once just warm, remove the cupcakes from the baking trays and leave to cool completely on a wire cooling rack.

TO DECORATE

1. Prepare a plastic piping bag fitted with a large star nozzle. Fill with the chilled frosting. Pipe a rosette of frosting on top of each cupcake.

HOLLY WILLOUGHBY

TV Presenter

Rich and Very Yummy Chocolate Cake

Food processor method

~ INGREDIENTS ~

- 180g plain flour

- 2 level tbsp cocoa

- 1 level tsp bicarbonate of soda

- 1 level tsp baking powder

- 140g caster sugar

- 2 level tbsp golden syrup

- 2 large eggs

- ¼ pint/5fl oz corn oil

- ¼ pint/5fl oz milk

ICING

- 55g butter

- 4 level tbsp cocoa

- 3 tbsp milk

- 140g icing sugar, sieved

~ METHOD ~

1. Grease and line 2x8in/20cm sandwich tins

2. Preheat oven to 170°C/325°F/Gas 3

3. In the bowl of the processor place the plain flour, cocoa, bicarbonate of soda and the baking powder. Add the caster sugar, syrup and eggs. Switch on and add the mixed oil and milk through the funnel, mix for 5 seconds until you have a dark batter. Turn into prepared tins and bake for 30–35 minutes before cooling on a wire rack.

4. To make the icing, melt the butter, add the cocoa and stir to blend. Cook for a minute. Stir in the milk and the icing sugar and mix till a smooth consistency. Leave to cool and thicken. Sandwich the cakes with half the icing and spread the remainder on top. Nice as it is but you can decorate with chocolate flake or grated chocolate.

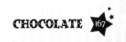

SAMANTHA PARK

Food Network UK Competition Winner

Chocolate Beetroot Cake

This recipe is inspired by the flavour of my favourite chocolate bar; Green & Black's Maya Gold.

INGREDIENTS

- 3 large eggs

- 200g soft light brown sugar

- 100g dark muscavado sugar

- 300ml sunflower oil

- 300g vacuum packed beetroot (without vinegar), drained

- 100g cocoa powder

- 1 heaped tsp allspice

- 200g plain flour

- 1 level tsp baking powder

- 1 level tsp bicarbonate of soda

- ½ tsp salt

- ½ tsp vanilla extract

- Grated zest of a large orange

- Damson jam (to fill the cake)

METHOD

1. Grease and line the bases of two 18cm (7") sandwich tins with baking paper.

2. Pre-heat the oven to 190°C (fan 180°C)

3. Using a food processor, blend the eggs, sugars and oil together until thick & creamy. Remove to a large mixing bowl.

4. Chop the beetroot into a smooth puree in the food processor.

5. Add the cocoa powder and allspice to the beetroot and blend together.

6. Add to the egg mixture and stir together.

7. Sift the dry ingredients into the bowl, adding the vanilla extract and orange zest and fold with a metal spoon until well incorporated.

8. Divide the mixture between the two sandwich tins and bake for approximately 35 minutes, or until an inserted cocktail stick comes out clean. The cakes will be quite dark in colour.

9. Leave to cool on wire racks.

10. When completely cold, sandwich together with damson jam (approx ½ a jar).

SERVES 8-10, DEPENDING ON HOW GENEROUS YOU LIKE YOUR SLICES!

Created by Samantha Park.

TARTS, PIES AND PUDDINGS

DEBBIE KINSELLA

Mother of Ben and Trustee of
The Ben Kinsella Trust

Ben's Traditional Apple Pie

~ INGREDIENTS ~

- 3 cooking apples
- 115g cooking margarine
- 225g plain flour
- 4 tbsp water
- 3 tbsp caster sugar
- Sprinkle of cinnamon
- 1 beaten egg

~ METHOD ~

1. Preheat oven to 220°C/425°F/Gas 7.

2. Put the margarine in a bowl and add the flour. Mix together until you have a crumbled mixture.

3. Add the water and mix it in with a knife. Mould into a ball, wrap in cling film and put it in the fridge to rest for 20 minutes.

4. Take out of fridge and roll out two thirds of the pastry to line the base and sides of the pie dish, using your rolling pin to pick up the pastry.

5. Trim off any excess pastry.

6. Peel, quarter and then slice the apples and create 3 layers in the pie dish, sprinkling each layer with a tbsp of sugar and dusting of cinnamon.

7. Dampen edges of pastry around the pie dish.

8. Roll out the remaining third of the pastry to make a top for the pie and attach to dampened edges, pressing together to form a pattern. Trim any excess pastry.

9. Using a fork, prick the pastry top twice to allow steam to escape.

10. Lightly brush the top with egg and cook in the oven for 10 minutes.

11. Reduce the heat to 190°C/375°F/Gas 5 for a further 30 minutes.

12. Take out of oven when golden brown and leave to cool for about 10 minutes before serving.

13. Can be eaten hot or cold with custard, cream or ice cream.

Photograph: Paul Grover/
Rex Features

SAMANTHA CAMERON

Figs with Barbados Cream

(With thanks to Nigella Lawson)
Barbados Cream is more like a great accompaniment than a
pudding – excellent with figs or other fruit.

INGREDIENTS

- Double cream
- Greek yoghurt
- Brown sugar
- Figs

METHOD

1. Take an equal amount of double cream and Greek yoghurt.

2. Whip the cream so it is stiff, like the yoghurt and then mix together.

3. Pour into a circular dish, 2 inches deep.

4. Sprinkle soft brown sugar evenly over the top.

5. Cover in cling film and leave in the fridge for over 4 hours.

6. Serve with quartered figs (or other fruit of choice) and enjoy!

JOANNA LUMLEY

Actress/Author

Fancy Bread and Butter Pudding

INGREDIENTS

- 50g butter

- 8 slices (1cm/½ in thick) of brioche loaf

- Small handful of sultanas soaked in cointreau or other orange-based liqueur

- 2 eggs

- 142ml/5fl oz carton double cream

- 225ml/8fl oz milk

- 1 tsp vanilla extract

- 2 tbsp caster sugar

~ METHOD ~

1. Heat oven to 160°C/325°F/Gas 3.

2. Soak the sultanas in the liqueur until soft.

3. Take a brioche loaf and slice into 1cm/½ in thick slices and butter lightly on one side and cut diagonally in half. Arrange in buttered dish with corners pointing upwards to give a nice effect when cooked. Do not remove crusts. Scatter the soaked sultanas in between the bread (and any remaining liqueur).

4. Whisk together the eggs, cream, milk, vanilla extract and sugar and pour over the buttered bread.

5. Next set the dish in a roasting tin and pour heated water around the dish to approx 2.5cm/1in depth. Bake in the centre of the oven for about 35 minutes until the top is browned and the 'custard' set.

6. This is delicious as it is or, alternatively with a dollop of whipped cream or home made vanilla ice cream.

PRUE LEITH
CBE

Chef/Author/Judge on
The Great British Menu

Normandy Tart

INGREDIENTS

FOR THE PASTRY

- 225g plain flour
- 140g butter
- 1 egg
- Pinch of salt
- 55g caster sugar

ALMOND FILLING

- 200g butter
- 200g caster sugar
- 200g ground almonds
- 2 eggs
- 2 extra yolks
- 1 tbsp calvados, kirsch, or whatever you like
- Few drops almond essence

TOPPING

- 3–5 eating apples
- Half a jar of apricot jam

METHOD

1. Set the oven at 200°C/400°F/Gas 6 and put a metal tray in it to heat.

2. Whizz everything together until the mix forms a ball. Roll out between two sheets of cling-film until big enough to line a 25cm/10in flan ring. Chill for 30 minutes. If the dish is porcelain, bake blind. If metal, don't bother.

3. Whizz almond filling in the food processor (no need to wash the bowl after pastry), then spread in the flan.

4. For the topping, 3 – 5 eating apples, depending on size Half a jar smooth apricot jam, warmed with a tbsp of water to a thick syrup. Peel the apples if you like, but no need. Core them and cut in half from top to stalk end. Slice each half-apple finely, keeping the slices in order. Arrange them on the filling.

5. Baking: Set the flan in the middle of the hot oven and bake for 15 minutes. Then paint with hot jam.

6. Turn the oven down to 180°C/350°F/Gas 4 and bake for half an hour or so until the filling is firm and brown. Remove from the oven and give it another brush with the jam if you think it needs it.

7. Serving: Best cooled to tepid or room temperature without refrigeration. If you make it in advance, freeze it and then reheat for 20 minutes at 180°C/350°F/Gas 4 and allow to cool. This will crisp up the pastry again.

ANGELA HARTNETT MBE

Chef/Author/Restaurateur

Lemon Meringue Pie

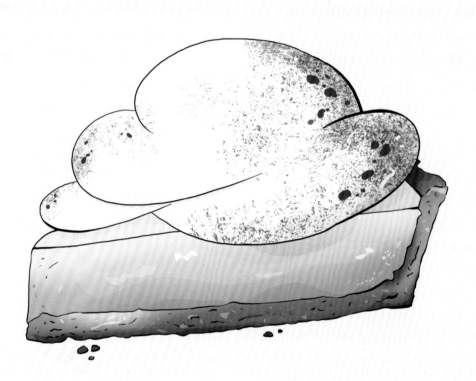

~ INGREDIENTS ~

SERVES 6-8

FOR THE LEMON BASE:

- 50g caster sugar
- 3 tbsp cornflour
- 275ml/9½ fl oz cold water
- Grated zest and juice of 2 lemons
- 2 eggs yolks
- 40g cold butter, diced

FOR THE MERINGUE TOPPING:

- 2 eggs whites
- 100g caster sugar

~ METHOD ~

1. Pre-heat the oven to 180°C/350°F/Gas 4.

2. Roll out the pastry and use to line a 25cm/10 in loose-bottomed flat tin. Place sheet of baking parchment inside and fill with baking beans, rice or dried pasta. Bake for 15 minutes. Remove the beans and parchment and bake for further 5 minutes.

3. Remove from the oven and leave to cool while prepare the filling.

4. Reduce the oven to 120°C/250°F/Gas 2.

5. To make the lemon base, put the sugar and the cornflour in a bowl and add enough of the water to make a smooth paste.

6. Put the remaining water in a medium pan with the lemon zest and juice and bring to the boil. Remove from the heat and add the cornflour mixture, stirring well. Return to the heat and bring to the boil again, then simmer for about 2 minutes, or until slightly thickened. Remove from the heat again and allow to cool slightly.

7. Add the egg yolks, one at a time, beating well after each addition.

8. Finally, beat in the butter. The mixture should be thick and glossy.

9. Pour into the baked pastry case and set aside while you make the meringue topping.

10. Put the egg whites in a large bowl and beat with an electric mixer until they form stiff peaks. Add the sugar a tablespoon at a time, whisking after each addition. When glossy, spoon on top of lemon mixture, using the back of a fork to form peaks.

11. Bake for about 20mins, or until meringue is golden brown. It may looked cracked on top, but do not worry - that's all part of its charm.

GIZZI ERSKINE

Food Writer/Chef/TV Presenter

Sticky Date
Banoffee Pudding

Adapted from Gizzi Erskine

INGREDIENTS

SERVES 6-8

- 250g chopped dates

- 250ml/9fl oz hot black tea, made with 1 teabag

- 1 tsp bicarbonate of soda

- 85g soft unsalted butter

- 175g caster sugar

- 2 large eggs

- 1 tsp good vanilla (if you don't have the good stuff, leave it out)

- 175g/1¼ cup) plain flour, sieved (I used ¼ cup stoneground wholemeal flour)

- 1 tsp baking powder

- Pinch of salt

- 3 bananas, roughly mashed

- 1 tsp ground cinnamon

- ¼ tsp nutmeg

- Vanilla ice cream, or mascarpone, to serve

CARAMEL/TOFFEE SAUCE

- 100g brown sugar (light or dark)

- 100g unsalted butter

- 150ml cream

METHOD

1. Pre-heat oven to 180°C/355°F/Gas 4. Butter a 23cm (9in) baking dish. I used an 8×8in brownie tin and loaf pan.

2. Place dates in a small pan and pour over hot tea. Boil for 3–4 minutes, until the dates have softened. Remove from heat, then stir in the bicarbonate of soda. It will fizz up. Set aside.

3. In a medium large bowl, beat butter and sugar until light and fluffy, then beat in eggs and vanilla, incorporating well after each addition. Fold in the flour, banana, mixed spice and the date mixture and pour into greased baking dish. Bake for 30–35 minutes, until a skewer or knife inserted in the centre comes out clean.

4. While the pudding is cooking, make the sauce. Put the sugar, butter and cream into a small saucepan, place over a low heat and melt until the sugar has dissolved. Then turn the heat up to medium high and simmer several minutes (it should bubble vigorously) until the sauce is darkened (a caramel colour if using light brown sugar, brown if using dark brown sugar).

5. Serve the cake drizzled with a spoonful of sauce and a scoop of vanilla ice cream or mascarpone. This is still incredibly good the next day, still soft and arguably more rich.

MICHEL ROUX JR

Chef/Author/Restaurateur

Pear and Roquefort Pie

~ INGREDIENTS ~

SERVES 8

- 6 pears Cornice or Conference peeled, cored and quartered

- 1 lemon

- 300g Roquefort cheese

- 500g puff pastry

- 1 whole egg

- 1 tablespoon butter

- 60g caster sugar

- Freshly ground black pepper

~ METHOD ~

1. Roll out the puff pastry on a lightly floured surface to 3mm thickness to a rectangle shape approximately 32x18cm cover and place on a baking sheet in the refrigerator.

2. Put the pears in a large pan over a medium heat with the butter, lightly cover with greaseproof paper and continue to cook until tender, turning the pieces occasionally over.

3. Remove the paper then add the sugar and turn-up the heat, once the sugar has caramelised pour in the lemon juice and season well with the black pepper. Take off the heat and leave to cool completely. Drain well and neatly place arrow of pears along one side of the puff pastry leaving a gap of 2cm on once side and 10cm on the other.

4. Crumb the Roquefort on the pears and then finish with the remaining pears. Now egg wash the sides using a pastry brush and fold the pastry over the pears, press down firmly to seal the edges then egg wash the outside. With the point of a knife, make 3 little holes on the top of the pie to enable the steam to escape, and then gently score the pastry to decorate.

5. Cook at 220°C/425°F/Gas 7 for 15 minutes then turn down the oven to 180°C and continue to cook for 20 minutes. Take out of the oven and place on a wire rack to cool. Only slice once completely cooled but not cold.

Recipe from Vin de Constance Cookbook

GILLIAN WRIGHT

Actress

Rosemary's Clootie Dumpling

Recipe handed down from my mum!
This is a traditional Scottish pudding with a modern twist (microwave cooked). It is usually served after Christmas dinner or at Hogmanay.

~ METHOD ~

1. Put water, sugar, mixed spice, cinnamon, fruit, margarine and treacle in a saucepan and bring contents to the boil. Simmer for one minute. Remove from the heat. When cooled, mix in the sieved flour and bicarbonate of soda then add the beaten eggs.

2. Pour the mixture into a large bowl suitable for microwave use, which has been lined with enough cling film to go over the sides. Do not cover the mixture with cling film. Cook in the microwave as detailed below. Turn out onto a plate and allow to cool before cutting.

3. Note: Cling film will be crinkly but this doesn't matter.

4. My bowl is 8½ in round and 3½ in deep.

5. 650 watt oven...9 minutes approx.

6. 800 watt oven...7.5 minutes approx.

7. Enjoy!

INGREDIENTS

- 300 ml/10fl oz /½ pint water
- 175g sugar
- 2 eggs beaten
- 225g plain flour, sifted
- 1 heaped tsp mixed spice
- 1 heaped tsp cinnamon
- 1 tsp bicarbonate of soda
- 115g margarine
- 225g mixed fruit
- 225g sultanas
- 1 tbsp treacle

DEAN EDWARDS

TV Chef

Apple Frangipane Tart

INGREDIENTS

SERVES 8

- 1 pack shop-bought short crust pastry

- 3 Braeburn apples peeled, cored and sliced

- 125g unsalted butter softened

- 2 eggs

- 125g caster sugar

- 125g ground almonds

- 20g plain flour

- 3 tbsp amaretto

- 2 tbsp marmalade, warmed

- Ice cream for serving

~ METHOD ~

1. Pre heat the oven to 180°C/350°F/Gas 4 . Roll the pastry out until ½cm/¼in thick and line a 23cm/9in loose-bottomed tart tin. Chill in the fridge for 1 hour. Prick the base with a fork, cover with baking parchment and pour in some ceramic baking beans. Then blind bake for 15 minutes. Remove the parchment and beans, then return to the oven for 10 minutes until crisp, remove from the oven and set aside to cool.

2. Cream the butter and caster sugar until light and fluffy, crack in the eggs one at a time, beating as you go. Sift in the almonds and flour then fold in until fully incorporated. Add the amaretto liquor and mix. Keep in the fridge until needed.

3. Spread the frangipane mixture into the pastry case then top with the sliced apples return to the oven and cook for a further 40–45 minutes or until golden. Brush the apples with the warmed marmalade to glaze. Slice and serve with some ice cream.

JUNE BROWN MBE

Actress - Dot in Eastenders

Dot's Banana and Coconut Pie

INGREDIENTS

- 225g short crust pastry
- Jam
- 2 Bananas
- Handful of desiccated coconut
- A little milk
- Sprinkling of caster sugar

METHOD

1. Take the short crust pastry and roll two thirds of the pastry into a circle. Spread a little jam in the centre, leaving two inches of bare pastry edges.

2. Chop up two bananas and place in the jam. Sprinkle with dessicated coconut, fold the bare edges of the pastry up round the slices of banana.

3. Roll out the remaining third of pastry, brushing this "smaller circle" with milk around the edges. Fit the smaller circle as a lid onto the larger pie.

4. Brush the top with milk and sprinkle with caster sugar. Bake for about 25minutes at 200°C/400°F/Gas 6.

5. I hope that this is of use to you and than anybody who likes the sound of it enjoys making it!

MARK SARGEANT

TV Chef/Author/Chef Patron,
Rocksalt, Folkestone

Gypsy Tart

Gypsy Tart is served at Rocksalt Restaurant, Folkestone

INGREDIENTS

● Sweet Pastry

● 2kg soft flour

● 1kg butter

● 1kg icing sugar

● 8 eggs

● 4 vanilla pods – seeds of

● Large pinch of salt

● Filling

● 340g dark muscovado sugar

● 410g evaporated milk

METHOD

1. Sieve the flour, salt and icing sugar into a large bowl. Rub in the cold diced butter until it forms breadcrumbs. Whisk together the eggs and vanilla seeds and pass through a fine sieve. Make a well in the flour mix then add the eggs. Mix together, then knead on a clean surface until the pastry comes together, cover and leave to set in the fridge for at least a couple of hours.

2. Roll out and place in a tart base tin, fully blind bake the tart case. Whisk the muscovado sugar and evaporated milk on a medium speed until thick. Pour straight into tart case and bake at 160°C/325°F/Gas 3 for 10 minutes. Take out of the oven and leave to cool before serving. Portion using a hot knife.

GABBY LOGAN

TV/Radio Presenter

Courgette Whoopie Pies

INGREDIENTS

- 2 cups plus 2 tbsp plain flour
- 1 tsp baking powder
- 1 tsp baking soda
- 1 tsp ground cinnamon
- ½ tsp nutmeg
- ½ tsp ground cloves
- 1 cup finely chopped nuts (optional)

- ½ tsp salt
- 1 cup granulated sugar
- ½ cup vegetable shortening
- 1 large egg
- 1 cup grated courgette-squeezed
- ½ cup milk
- 1 tsp vanilla extract

FILLING

- 4 oz cream cheese, softened
- 2oz unsalted butter, softened
- 2¼ cups icing sugar
- ½ tsp pure vanilla extract
- Scant ¼ teaspoon salt

METHOD

FOR THE PIES

1. Mix shortening and sugar. Add in egg. Mix. Add milk and mix.

2. Add in dry ingredients and stir.

3. Blend in the courgette and vanilla.

4. Bake on a greased cookie sheet at 180°C/350°/Gas 4 for about 12–15 minutes, until the bottom gets browned.

5. Cool and sandwich cookies with cream cheese filling.

FOR THE FILLING

1. Beat all ingredients together until light and fluffy.

NICKI WATERMAN

Fitness Expert and TV Health Guru

Blackberry and Apple Layer

INGREDIENTS

- 450g Bramley apples, peeled, cored and sliced

- 125g blackberries

- 75g soft brown sugar

- Juice ½ lemon

- 15g butter

- 50g chopped toasted almonds

- 90ml Alpro soya vanilla dessert, chilled

~ METHOD ~

1. Place the apples, blackberries, sugar and lemon juice in a saucepan. Cover and simmer, stirring occasionally until apples and blackberries have turned to a thick pulp. Remove from the heat and allow to cool.

2. Melt the butter in a frying pan and cook the breadcrumbs, stirring occasionally until golden and crisp. Remove from the heat and stir in the chopped nuts. Allow to cool.

3. Spoon half the apple puree into four glasses. Top with the vanilla cream and sprinkle over the nut mixture. Chill until ready to serve.

HEALTH TIP: This is a tasty pudding, ideal for anti-aging as it contains antioxidants. The dairy products used are also a great way to increase your calcium intake, therefore helping to prevent osteoporosis.

Photograph: Paul
Winch-Furness

PAUL A. YOUNG

Chocolatier/Patissier

Sweet Potato, Cream Cheese and Chocolate Fudge Tart

~ INGREDIENTS ~

**MAKES ONE
8IN/20CM ROUND
TART**

FOR THE CRUST

- 165g soft unsalted butter

- 75g unrefined light muscovado sugar

- 2 free range egg yolks

- 250g plain flour

- 1 tsp sea salt

**FOR THE SWEET
POTATO FILLING**

- 6 medium sized sweet potatoes

- 50g full fat cream cheese

- Half a vanilla pod split and deseeded

**FOR THE CHOCOLATE
FUDGE LAYER**

- 100g unsalted butter

- 100g unrefined light muscovado sugar

- 100ml double cream

- 5g sea salt

- 100g of your favourite fine quality dark chocolate chopped into small even sized pieces – I use Duffy's 70% Star of Peru or Willies Peruvian 70%

FOR DECORATION

- Lots of dark chocolate to cut in to shards

- Cocoa powder for light dusting

METHOD

1. To make the crust – Cream together the butter and sugar with a wooden spoon until light and creamy. Add the egg yolks, 20ml cold water mixing very well until smooth and glossy. Gradually add the flour and salt until a soft paste is formed. Wrap the paste in cling film and pop in the fridge for one hour to harden.

2. To line your tart ring, sprinkle a little flour onto your surface and knead the dough for 30 seconds until smooth and pliable. Roll out until 3mm thick and 5cm larger than your tart ring. Using the rolling pin lift the paste in to the tart ring and carefully press into the base and edges being careful not to puncture the paste. Do not trim the excess paste off just yet. Place in the refrigerator for 30 minutes.

> I love combining traditionally savoury ingredients with sweet and especially with chocolate. The balance of salty and sweet can be so moreish and enticing. I came across chocolate fudge and sweet potato as a combination and just had to make it in a tart.

3. Meanwhile bake your sweet potatoes for 45 minutes at 180°C/350°F/Gas 4 or until they are very soft. Cut in half and scoop out the flesh. Mash well with the back of a fork and place in a sieve then with a wooden spoon and a circular motion push the flesh though the sieve into a mixing bowl. Add the cream cheese, vanilla seeds and mix well. Place aside for later.

4. Now to blind bake the tart case by lining the tart with 4 layers of cling film then either uncooked rice, lentils or baking beans and fold the excess cling film into the centre, bake for 20 minutes at 175°C/325°/Gas 3. Open the oven and carefully lift out the baking beans in their cling film and pop back in the oven for 5 minutes to brown the base.

5. Remove from the oven and spread the sweet potato onto the base of the tart.

6. To make the fudge place the butter, sugar and salt into a medium sauce pan and bring the boil, time 10 minutes then remove from the heat, add the cream taking care as it can splutter at this stage, whisk well then add the chopped dark chocolate mixing until all the chocolate has melted.

7. Pour the fudge over the sweet potato layer, any fudge left over can be put in a jam jar and spread on crumpets of warmed and poured over ice cream.

8. Allow the tart to cool and refrigerate for two hours.

9. Now with a serrated knife trim off any excess paste from around the tart ring.

10. Present the tart on a favourite plate or cake stand ready to decorate.

11. For the decoration simply chop the chocolate in to shards and pile up over the tart and sift a small amount of cocoa over the chocolate.

12. Serve at room temperature.

ANDREA MCLEAN

TV Presenter

Pancakes

My favourite for Saturday mornings or anytime.

~ METHOD ~

1. Mix ingredients together and pour a bit at a time into pan.

2. Delicious with maple syrup and strawberries.

INGREDIENTS

- 1 teacup flour

- 1 teacup milk

- 1 egg

- Pinch of cinnamon

- Butter or margarine for frying

GINO D'ACAMPO

TV Chef/Author/Presenter of
ITV1 Let's Do Lunch with Gino and Mel

Doppio Cioccolato con Pistacchio

(Double chocolate mousse with Pistachio nuts)

~ METHOD ~

1. Melt the chocolate in a glass bowl over a pan with hot water (don't let the bowl touch the water). Once melted, set aside to cool, but not to harden.

2. Beat the eggs and sugar in a bowl until thick and pale. With the help of a metal spoon fold the chocolate into the egg mixture. Add in the nuts and amaretto liquor, mix well and then gently fold in the whipped cream.

3. Place the mixture into four separate dessert glasses (approx. 250ml), refrigerate for 3 hours until set. Just before serving decorate with some crushed pistachio nuts on top.

INGREDIENTS

SERVES 4

● 150g dark chocolate (good quality and chopped)

● 100g white chocolate (good quality and chopped)

● 3 fresh eggs

● 2 tbsp caster sugar

● 2 tbsp amaretto liquor

● 250ml/9fl oz softly whipped cream

● 2 handfuls crushed pistachio nuts

CHRIS GALVIN

TV Chef/Restaurateur

Lemon Tart

~ INGREDIENTS ~

SERVES: 8

- 1 quantity of sweet shortcrust pastry

- 2 free-range egg yolks, beaten

- Icing sugar, to dust

FOR THE LEMON FILLING

- Finely grated zest and juice of 10 unwaxed lemons (you need 450ml/16fl oz juice)

- 500g caster sugar

- 1l/1¾ pints double cream

- 6 free-range eggs

- 6 free-range egg yolks

~ METHOD ~

1. Roll the pastry out on a lightly floured work surface, then use it to line a 25cm/10in loose-bottomed flan tin about 4.5cm/1¾in deep, or a cake ring placed on a baking tray lined with baking parchment. Leave the excess pastry overhanging the edge of the tin as this will be trimmed after cooking.

2. Refrigerate for 25 minutes.

3. Line the pastry case with greaseproof paper, then fill to the top with baking beans (if you don't have baking beans, use plain uncooked beans or rice). Bake in an oven preheated to 180°C/350°F/Gas 4 for 18–20 minutes or until pale golden.

4. Remove from the oven and lift out the paper and beans, then return the pastry case to the oven and bake for a further 4 minutes.

5. Remove from the oven again and brush the egg yolks over the hot pastry case.

6. Return to the oven for 2 minutes, then transfer to a wire rack. Reduce the oven temperature to 110°C/225°F/Gas ¼.

7. To make the filling, put the lemon juice and caster sugar in a pan and bring to the boil over a medium heat, stirring occasionally. Remove from the heat, stir in the lemon zest and leave to infuse for 3–4 minutes, then pass the mixture through a fine sieve.

8. Put the cream in a separate pan and bring to the boil, then remove from the heat and leave to cool slightly.

9. Put the eggs and egg yolks into a large mixing bowl and whisk together, then, whilst still whisking, pour the lemon juice/sugar mixture on to the eggs. Whisk in the cream, then pass the mixture through a fine sieve. Skim off any bubbles from the top.

10. Place the pastry case in the tin on a baking sheet and place this on the shelf in the oven, then gently pour in the lemon filling, taking it to the very top and being very careful to avoid any spillages. Bake for about 40 minutes or until only just set. The middle should wobble like a jelly when the tart is cooked.

11. Remove from the oven and leave the tart to cool on the baking sheet for at least 3 hours at room temperature–do not put it in the fridge as the pastry will go soggy.

12. When cool, neatly trim off the excess pastry from around the edge of the tart using a small paring knife. Carefully remove the tart from the tin or ring, then cut it into wedges. Dust with icing sugar and caramelize the top with a chef's blowtorch just before serving.

KERI-ANNE PAYNE

British Olympic Swimmer,
Team GB 2012

Aunty Hill's Milk Tart

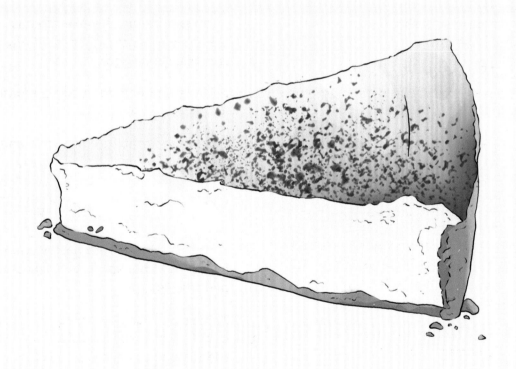

INGREDIENTS

PASTRY

- 55g butter
- 85g caster sugar
- ½ egg
- 115g plain flour
- 1 tsp baking powder
- Pinch of salt

FILLING

- 475ml/17fl oz whole milk
- ½ tsp vanilla extract
- ½ tbsp butter
- 1¼ tbsp flour
- 1 tbsp cornflour
- 50g caster sugar
- 1 egg, beaten
- Cinnamon for dusting

METHOD

1. Pre-heat oven to 180°C/350°F/Gas 4.

2. Lightly grease a shallow 23cm/9in pie pan or tart tin.

3. In a large mixing bowl or food processor, cream the butter and the sugar.

4. Add the egg and mix well.

5. Sieve the flour, baking powder and salt together and add to the creamed mixture until thoroughly combined.

6. Press this into the prepared pie pan or tart tin and bake for about 10-15 minutes until golden brown. Remove from oven and let cool in dish.

7. In a large saucepan, combine milk, vanilla extract and ½ tbsp. butter.

8. Bring to boil over medium heat and then remove from hob.

9. In a separate bowl, while the milk is heating, mix together the flour, cornflour and sugar.

10. Add the beaten egg to sugar mixture and whisk until smooth.

11. Slowly whisk mixture into milk and return pan to heat and bring to a boil, stirring constantly for about 3–5 minutes until it starts to thicken and then remove from heat.

12. Pour this mixture into pastry shell and finish off with a sprinkle of cinnamon over the top.

13. This dessert can be served warm or cold but I prefer it cold from the fridge, with a great cup of coffee.

ATUL KOCHHAR

Chef/Restaurateur

Fennel Bread and Butter Pudding with Ginger Custard

~ INGREDIENTS ~

PUDDING

- 500g milk
- 175g egg
- 100g granulated sugar
- 100g unsalted butter
- 8 slices of brioche bread (edges cut)
- 20g fennel

GINGER CUSTARD

- 250g milk
- 250g double cream
- 80g egg yolk
- 75g granulated sugar
- 2 vanilla pod scraps
- 30g ginger

GINGER BISCUIT

- 240g sugar
- 120g golden syrup
- 120g unsalted butter
- 50g egg
- 360g plain flour
- 30g ginger powder
- 5g cinnamon powder
- 5g bicarbonate of soda

~ METHOD ~

PUDDING

1. Boil the milk with fennel and leave to infuse for 3 hours.

2. Strain the milk and add the egg and sugar to make a custard.

3. Butter brioche slices and arrange in tin foil-lined baking pan.

4. Pour over half the custard and leave for half an hour for bread to soak the mix

5. Pour the remaining mix into the pan and place the remaining butter evenly on top.

6. Bake the pudding

GINGER CUSTARD

1. Boil milk, cream, vanilla pod and scrap together.

2. Infuse with the ginger (coarsely cut) for 3 hours.

3. Strain the mixture.

4. Whisk the yolk and sugar together till peaks appear then temper with the hot milk mixture.

5. Make the custard over a slow heat, stirring constantly, check with back of the spoon for consistency

GINGER BISCUIT

1. Cream the sugar, golden syrup and butter together.

2. Add the egg.

3. Fold in dry ingredients.

4. Spread evenly on a parchment paper using rolling pin and cut into bars.

5. Bake at 100°C/225°F/Gas ¼ for 20 minutes.

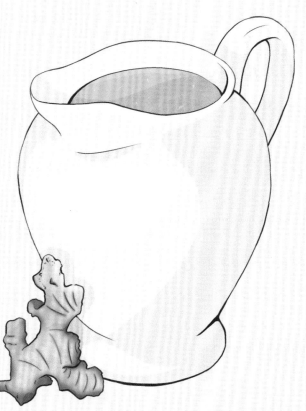

Photograph: Adam
Lawrence

ANITA RANI

Television Presenter, Winner of The Great
Sport Relief Bake Off, 2012

Pineapple and Blackberry Coconut Crumble Boom!

~ INGREDIENTS ~

- 125g Plain Flour
- 25g ground almonds
- 25g desiccated coconut
- 25g caster sugar
- 25g demerara sugar
- large handful of oats
- 100g chilled unsalted butter in cubes
- 50ml/2fl oz dark rum
- 1½ tsp ginger powder
- Extra demerara sugar for pineapple
- 1 large ripe pineapples
- 1 punnet blackberries

~ METHOD ~

1. Preheat oven to 180°C/350°F/Gas 4.

2. Peel and cube the pineapple, remember to remove the hard bit in the middle.

3. Toss in brown sugar and ginger, then fry in three batches using a hot frying pan.

4. Pour a third of the rum over and quickly light with a match. Keep eyebrows out of the way!

5. Repeat until all done. Put into dish. Add Blackberries evenly over the top.

6. Put flour, almonds and butter in bowl and rub to make breadcrumbs. There can be butter lumps in it. No worries.

7. Add the caster and demerara sugar, the desiccated coconut and the oats.

8. Mix it all up.

9. Put onto the fruit. Don't pat down.

10. Cover all holes.

11. Put into oven and bake for 35–40 minutes.

RT HON HARRIET HARMAN MP

Deputy Leader of the Labour Party/Shadow Secretary of State for Culture, Media and Sport

From "Nigella Bites"
by Nigella Lawson

Sticky Toffee Pudding

INGREDIENTS

SERVES: 6–8

FOR THE CAKE

- 100g dark muscovado sugar
- 175g self-raising flour
- 125ml full-fat milk

- 1 egg
- 1 teaspoon vanilla extract
- 50g unsalted butter, melted
- 200g chopped, rolled dates

FOR THE SAUCE

- 200g dark muscovado sugar
- Approx. 25g unsalted butter in little blobs
- 500ml boiling water

METHOD

1. Preheat the oven to 190°C/375°F/Gas 5 and butter a 1½-litre capacity pudding dish.

2. Combine the 100g dark muscovado sugar with the flour in a large bowl.

3. Pour the milk into a measuring jug, beat in the egg, vanilla and melted butter and then pour this mixture over the sugar and flour, stirring – just with a wooden spoon – to combine. Fold in the dates then scrape into the prepared pudding dish. Don't worry if it doesn't look very full: it will do by the time it cooks.

4. Sprinkle over the 200g dark muscovado sugar and dot with the butter. Pour over the boiling water (yes really!) and transfer to the oven. Set the timer for 45 minutes, though you might find the pudding needs 5 or 10 minutes more. The top of the pudding should be springy and spongy when it's cooked; underneath, the butter, dark muscovado sugar and boiling water will have turned into a rich, sticky sauce. Serve with vanilla ice cream, creme fraiche, double or single cream as you wish.

ADAM BYATT

TV Chef/Author/Chef Patron, Trinity
Restaurant, Clapham, London

Baked Alaska

~ INGREDIENTS ~

MAKES: 6

- 500ml/18fl oz strawberry sorbet
- 500ml/18 fl oz vanilla ice cream
- 5 egg whites

- 280g caster sugar
- 50ml brandy/2fl oz (optional)

SPONGE

- vegetable oil, for brushing

- 250g caster sugar
- 250g butter
- 3 eggs
- 250g plain flour
- 2 tsp baking powder

~ METHOD ~

PREPARATION

1. Preheat the oven to 180°C/350°F/160°C fan/Gas 4.

2. Brush the inside of a 30cm x 23cm x 6cm cake tin with oil and line the bottom with parchment paper.

3. Make the sponge. Put all the ingredients into a food processor and blend well for 4 minutes. Pour into the cake tin and bake for 25 minutes. Remove the sponge from the cake tin and cool on a wire rack.

4. Split the cooled sponge horizontally into 3 equal layers.

TOP TIP Once the Alaska is piped with the meringue, it will happily sit in the freezer for a few days, but it is delicate and needs to be stored carefully in a large airtight container.

BAKING

1. Remove the sorbet and ice cream from the freezer and allow to soften slightly.

2. Put one of the sponge layers on an ovenproof serving dish and spread the sorbet over it. Cover with another layer of sponge and spread the ice cream over this, then top with the final layer of sponge. Trim the sides to form a neat rectangle, and place in the freezer. Leave for at least 45 minutes, to firm up the layers.

3. Preheat the oven to 220°C/425°F/200°C fan/Gas 7.

4. Put the egg whites and one-quarter of the sugar into a bowl and begin whisking with an electric mixer on medium speed. After 10 minutes or so, add another quarter of the sugar and continue whisking. Now gradually add the remaining sugar, whisking all the time until the whites are glossy and firm and the bowl can be turned upside down without the whites falling out. This will take about 15 minutes in total.

5. Using a piping bag (or a plastic sandwich bag with one of the bottom corners cut off), pipe the meringue over the sponge and ice cream to cover them completely, in as decorative a manner as you fancy.

6. Place the whole dish in the oven and bake for 3 minutes, until the meringue turns golden brown.

7. If you opt for the flaming version, you will need to warm the brandy in a small pan before pouring it over the Alaska and igniting it.

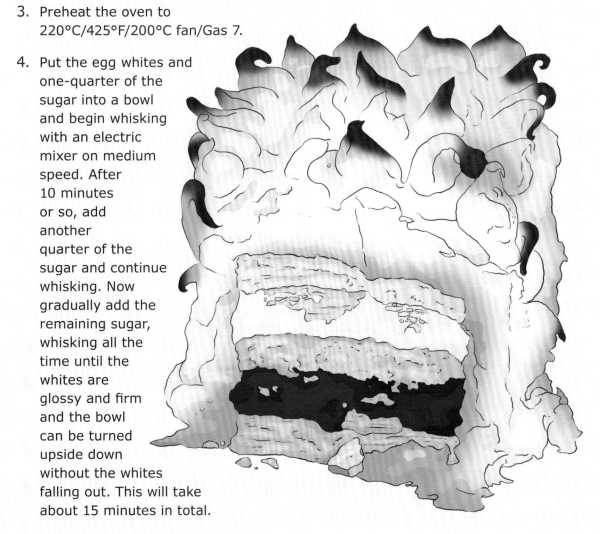

JASON ATHERTON

Chef Patron, Pollen Street Social, London

Malva Pudding

~ INGREDIENTS ~

SERVES 6

- 200g caster sugar
- 1 egg
- 15ml soft butter, plus extra for the baking dish
- 30ml smooth apricot jam

- 120g cake flour
- 5ml bicarb of soda
- 1ml salt
- 15ml wine vinegar
- 5ml vanilla extract
- Icing sugar, for sifting

- Softly whipped cream, to serve

SAUCE

- 250ml cream or evaporated milk
- 100g unsalted butter
- 125ml sugar

~ METHOD ~

1. Heat the oven to 180°C/350°F/Gas 4. Butter a 2-litre oven-to-table baking dish.

2. Beat together the caster sugar, egg, butter and jam until pale and fluffy.

3. Sift together the flour, bicarb and salt.

4. Mix together the milk, vinegar and vanilla extract.

5. Fold alternatively into the egg mixture until thoroughly mixed.

6. Pour batter into baking dish and bake for about 45 minutes until firm.

SAUCE

1. While the pudding is baking, combine the sauce ingredients in a small saucepan.

2. Heat, stirring, until the butter melts and has dissolved into caramel.

3. Pour over the pudding as it comes out of the oven. Set aside for about 15 minutes to allow the pudding to absorb the sauce.

4. Serve warm from the baking dish, or cut into squares and arrange on a plate. Sift over a cloud of icing sugar and offer with whipped cream.

PEARL LOWE

Singer/Designer

Spicy Plum Crumble

This recipe is by James Martin from his book Desserts

INGREDIENTS

- 50g butter

- 15 fresh dark plums, halved, stones removed

- 1 vanilla pod, split in half

- 1 star anise

- Pinch freshly grated

nutmeg

- 2 cinnamon sticks

- 50ml/1¾ fl oz water

- 100ml/3½ fl oz red wine

- 5 tbsp golden syrup

- 4 tbsp caster sugar

CRUMBLE TOPPING

- 190g plain flour

- 100g demerara sugar

- 100g butter, softened

TO SERVE

- Ice cream or double cream

METHOD

1. Preheat the oven to 200°C/400°F/Gas 6.

2. Heat the butter in a large pan over a medium heat. Add the plums and fry for a few minutes.

3. Add the split vanilla pod, star anise, nutmeg and cinnamon sticks to the pan. Add the water, red wine, golden syrup and sugar and bring to the boil. Reduce the heat and simmer for 6–8 minutes, until the plums break down to a thick sauce.

4. Transfer the plum mixture to a deep ovenproof dish.

5. For the crumble topping, mix the flour and sugar together in a bowl. Rub in the butter with your fingers until the mixture resembles breadcrumbs.

6. Sprinkle the crumble over the plums and bake in the oven for 20–25 minutes, until golden-brown.

7. Remove and allow to cool slightly before serving with ice-cream or double cream.

HAYLEY TAMADDON

Actress/Winner of Dancing on Ice 2010

Apple Crumble

INGREDIENTS

- 4 medium cooking apples
- 170g granulated sugar
- 170g butter or cooking margarine
- 280g self-raising flour
- Hayley's secret ingredient... Three quarters of a teaspoon of cinnamon

~ METHOD ~

Turn your oven on at the very beginning so that it's pre-heated ready to cook later on!!

1. Heat settings are 180°C/350°F/Gas 5.

2. Now as for making the crumble... The electric blender and fork can stay in the drawer. It's all about your HANDS getting involved.

3. Mix the butter/ margarine with the flour until you have a texture like breadcrumbs.

4. Next- pop in 4 of the 6 ounces of sugar to the mixture and give your hands some more exercise mixing that in.

5. Now it's time to tackle the apples. Peel them and chop them into 4 parts, cutting out the nasty core. Then chop your apple quarters into even smaller sections. I like them to be quite thin so i usually cut them into 6 slices.

6. Put your apples into the casserole dish and bosh in the secret cinnamon as well as your last 2 ounces of sugar.

7. Now add your crumble mixture and you're ready to glide over to the oven... put it in for 40 minutes.

8. To add some authenticity to your new found 'Baking Fairy' status put the apple crumble under a hot grill for about 30 seconds to 'brown' the crumple topping! Keep a close eye on it though. Black crumble topping will make you regret the decision to show off!

9. Leave it to cool for 15 minutes. Apple crumble can remain hot for quite a while and after all that hard work you want to have a mouth full of yumminess rather than your taste buds being burnt off.

10. Then the only important decision left to make is whether you fancy it with ice cream, cream or CUSTARD!!

TOM AND HENRY HERBERT

The Fabulous Baker Brothers
TV Bakers/Chefs/Authors

Steamed Date and Walnut Pudding

This pudding is based on Sodbury cake, a heritage recipe of ours, one we've made for generations in the bakery. We were approached a few years ago by Highgrove, Prince Charles's residence, asking for the recipe for a book they were doing. Apparently it was the Queen Mother's favourite, and whenever she came to Highgrove, which is not far from our bakery, she requested it. It was our old family favourite for decades, and now we know it was the Queen Mother's too. We were totally chuffed to be asked – but we didn't give them the recipe. This recipe isn't for Sodbury cake, but it's pretty damned close. And as a pudding, it's better. Sasha Jenner, Hobbs House original patisserie chef, came up with this version.

~ INGREDIENTS ~

- Butter for greasing
- 175g self-raising flour
- 75g vegetable suet
- 2 tbsp sugar
- 50g dark molasses
- 100g chopped dates
- 100g chopped walnuts

- The zest of one lemon
- Pinch of salt
- 1 egg
- 150ml/5fl oz milk

FOR THE STICKY TOFFEE SAUCE

- 80g butter

- 1 tbsp soft brown sugar
- 1 tbsp molasses
- 2 tbsp double cream
- Zest of one lemon
- Shot of whisky, brandy or Armagnac
- Chopped walnuts

~ METHOD ~

1. Butter a 850ml/1½ pint pudding bowl.

2. Put all the ingredients except the egg and the milk in a mixing bowl and mix together well.

3. Beat the egg into the milk in a jug and then stir into the cake mixture. The result should be of a loose, dropping consistency. Pour it into the pudding bowl.

4. Cut a disc of greaseproof paper large enough to fit the top of the pudding; then cut a second, larger disc and put that, with a pleat in it, right over the top so it overhangs the sides. Tie it in place with kitchen string, place in a large pan and pour in boiling water until it comes just over halfway up the sides of the bowl. If you tie the string around the pudding and over the top to make a handle, you've got a convenient way to get the pudding out.

5. Bring to the boil and simmer for 2½ hours. Check periodically that it has not boiled dry. Invert onto a large plate to serve.

FOR THE STICKY TOFFEE SAUCE

1. Put all the above ingredients in a small saucepan and bring to the boil whilst stirring.

2. Pour over the pudding just before serving and scatter with chopped walnuts.

ANDY BATES

Food Network UK Chef

White Chocolate and Raspberry Tart

INGREDIENTS

FOR THE PASTRY

- 2 cups plain flour, plus extra for dusting
- ¾ cup icing sugar
- Pinch of salt

- 5oz butter
- 1 large egg
- 1 egg yolk

FOR THE FILLING

- 300g white chocolate
- 300ml/10fl oz single cream
- 60ml /2¼ fl oz whole milk
- 2 eggs
- 600g fresh raspberries
- Icing sugar to dust

~ METHOD ~

1. Pre-heat the oven to 180°C/350°F/ Gas 4.

2. To make the pastry, mix together the flour, icing sugar and salt in a food processor. Add the butter and blend until the mixture resembles breadcrumbs. Mix in a little of the beaten egg at a time, until the pastry forms a ball, you may not need all the egg. Wrap tightly in cling-film and refrigerate for 1 hour. The pastry can be frozen and used at a later date.

3. Remove the pastry from the cling-film and roll out onto a lightly floured surface to 0.1 in/2.5mm in thickness. Line a 10 in/25 cm tart ring with the pastry, making sure to let the pastry hang over the side – the excess will fall off during cooking. Place it on a baking sheet and put it in the fridge for 30 minutes.

4. Line the pastry with greaseproof paper and fill with baking beans to keep the base's shape, and bake blind for about 20 minutes. Remove the baking beans and greaseproof paper and return to the oven for a further 5-8 minutes or until the pastry is starting to turn golden brown. Don't allow it to get

too much color as it will be returning to the oven for a further 40 minutes of cooking with the custard. Remove from the oven, brush with egg yolk and place in the oven for a further 5 minutes. Remove from the oven and leave to cool completely. Turn the oven down to 150°C/300°F/Gas 2

5. For the filling, break the chocolate into pieces put into a bowl and set aside. Bring the cream and milk to the boil and pour it over the chocolate pieces. Stir well until the chocolate and cream are mixed. Allow to cool for 5 minutes. Beat the eggs, then add to the chocolate and mix well.

6. Fill the pastry case with the chocolate custard. Carefully place in the middle of the oven and bake for 40-50 minutes or until the custard appears set. Remove from the oven and allow to cool to room temperature. Rest in the fridge until completely set.

7. Carefully, starting from the outside edge, cover the tart with the raspberries working towards the middle. Carefully dust the tart with icing sugar before serving.

GOK WAN

Fashion Consultant & TV Presenter

Red Bean Bao

~ INGREDIENTS ~

MAKES ABOUT 8

INGREDIENTS FOR THE BUNS

- 500g plain flour, plus a little extra for dusting
- 1 sachet (7g) of fast-action yeast
- 2 tbsps groundnut oil
- 2 tbsps caster sugar
- 300ml warm water
- 1 tbsp sesame oil

INGREDIENTS FOR BAO FILLING:

- ½ jar red bean paste

TO GARNISH

- 16 goji berries

~ METHOD ~

1. Put all the ingredients for the buns apart from the water and sesame oil into a bowl and roughly combine. Pour half the warm water into the dry ingredients and stir. Pour in the remaining water and mix well. Dust a clean surface with a little of the extra flour, and tip the dough onto it. Knead with your hands for five minutes. Once kneaded, if possible try to shape your dough into a rough 'bun'.

2. Rub the inside of a large bowl with the sesame oil. Put in your dough, cover with cling film or a clean tea towel, place in a warm place and leave to prove until the dough has at least doubled in size. This normally takes a minimum of 90 minutes.

3. Tip the dough onto a floured surface and knead again to knock out the air. Take a golf-ball sized piece of dough and flatten with the palm of your hand. Spoon at least one and a half tsps of the red bean paste into the middle of the flattened pastry. Carefully pull up the edges of the dough to encase the filling in a ball shape, then smooth the edges and place on a floured tray.

4. Repeat the process with the remaining dough and filling, then cover the buns with a damp tea towel and leave to rise for another 15 minutes. Once risen, place each one on a small disc of baking parchment with the join underneath. Top each bun with two goji berries. Place in a steamer and cook for 12-15 minutes. Once cooked serve immedlately, and there you have it your very own Chinese Red Bean Bao!

VALENTINE WARNER

TV Chef/Author

Treacle Tart

Taken from The Good Table by Valentine Warner, published by Mitchell Beazley

~ INGREDIENTS ~

SERVES 10–12

- 4 medium free-range eggs
- 907g can golden syrup
- Juice and finely grated zest of 1 small unwaxed lemon
- 225g white breadcrumbs, made from a 1–2 day-old loaf (crusts removed)
- Clotted cream, to serve

PASTRY

- 250g plain flour, plus extra for dusting
- 1 tbsp caster sugar
- 150g butter, chilled, cut into 2cm dice
- 1 medium free-range egg, beaten

~ METHOD ~

1. To make the filling, put the eggs in a large bowl and whisk lightly.

2. Stir in the syrup, lemon juice and zest, followed by the breadcrumbs. Set aside.

3. While the pastry case is prepared. This will give the breadcrumbs time to absorb the syrup.

4. To make the pastry, put the flour, sugar and butter in a food processor and blend on the pulse setting until the mixture resembles fine breadcrumbs.

5. With the motor running, slowly add the beaten egg and blend for just long enough for the mixture to form a ball.

6. Transfer to a lightly floured work surface and roll out to around 3mm thick, turning the pastry and flouring the surface regularly.

7. Use to line a 25cm/10 inch loose based fluted tart tin. Make sure the pastry is tucked into the corner of the tin.

8. Trim the edges neatly, prick the base lightly with a fork and chill the pastry for 30 minutes. Preheat the oven to 200°C/400°F/Gas 6.

9. Put the pastry case on a baking tray and line with crumpled baking paper.

10. Fill with baking beans. Bake blind for 20 minutes, then carefully take out of the oven and remove the baking paper and beans.

11. Return to the oven for a further 5–6 minutes, or until the base of the tart has darkened in colour and looks crisp and dry. Remove from the oven and reduce the temperature to 180°C/350°F/Gas 4.

12. Pour the syrup mixture into the tart case. Bake for 35–40 minutes, or until the filling is pale golden brown. Leave in the tin for 30 minutes, then remove.

13. Cut into slender wedges to serve with clotted cream.

RUSSELL GRANT

Astrologer and contestant on
Strictly Come Dancing 2011

Coconut Cream Pie

INGREDIENTS

- 375g ready rolled sweet shortcrust pastry
- 225g caster sugar
- 70g plain flour
- 1 tsp salt
- 600ml + 125ml/1 pint + 4fl oz lukewarm whole milk
- 3 egg yolks
- 2 tbsp butter
- 1 tsp vanilla essence
- 70g desiccated coconut

METHOD

1. Pre-heat oven to very hot 230°C/450°F/Gas 8.

2. Lightly grease a 23cm/9in pie dish with 1 tbsp butter.

3. Roll out pastry into a circle about 35cm/14in in diameter and about 8mm/⅛in thick. Lift with rolling pin and unroll it over pie dish and line it, trimming off excess dough so that it is even with outer rim of pie dish.

4. Crimp edge of dough and prick the bottom and sides of the dough.

5. Bake in oven for 15 minutes or until pastry is golden, and then remove it to cool down.

6. Put sugar, flour and salt in a medium sized saucepan and mix well.

7. Stirring continuously with a wooden spoon, pour in the lukewarm milk in a thin stream and place pan over low heat to cook for about 10 minutes or until the mixture thickens.

8. Remove from heat and cool for 5 minutes.

9. In a small bowl, beat the egg yolks with a fork and then add 3 tbsp of thickened milk mixture to the eggs and stir well.

10. Pour egg mixture in a thin stream into remaining milk mixture and replace pan on heat and cook for a further 3 minutes, stirring continuously until mixture is quite thick.

11. Remove pan from heat and stir in butter, vanilla and all but 2 tbsp of coconut.

12. Spoon the mixture into baked pastry case.

13. Sprinkle the remaining coconut on top and bake in oven for 15 minutes or until lightly browned.

14. Remove pie from oven and let it cool completely before serving.

NICHOLA SMITH

Chef

Sea-buckthorn Posset and Fig Tart

Sea-buckthorn is a plant found along the English coast line and if it wasn't so laborious to harvest (due to it's hostile spikes), I'm sure we would be using the stunning golden berries of this plant more often. It has a very distinctive flavour and is packed full of healing properties, it's healthy and it's yummy!

I have purchased my Sea-buckthorn from Miles Irving at Forager (forager@btconnect.com / 01227 732322), where it is sold already juiced by the litre. This recipe only requires a small amount, so I either freeze the rest or make lovely presses/cordials for summer time consumption. However, lemon or lime will make a great posset too.

INGREDIENTS

Will make one large tart or 24 tartlets

FOR THE PASTRY

- 225g organic plain flour

- 80g unrefined caster sugar

- 110g cold butter cubed

- Zest of one lemon

- 1 large free range egg

- Little milk

FOR THE POSSET

- 600ml/1 pint

double cream

- 150g unrefined sugar

- 100ml/3 ½fl oz sea-buckthorn juice

- (If using lemon, use the juice of 2)

- 6 ripe figs

- Icing sugar to dust

~ METHOD ~

FOR PASTRY

1. Pre heat oven to 180°C/350°F/Gas Mark 4.

2. In a large bowl sieve flour and mix in sugar.

3. Using your hands rub in the butter until you have a crumb like texture and no big buttery lumps left.

4. Add the lemon zest and mix.

5. Gently work in the egg and a little milk, just enough to form a dough.

6. DO NOT OVER WORK, this will ruin the pastry and make it shrink when cooking. You want it nice and short, so best to under work than over.

7. Wrap the pastry in cling film and refrigerate for half an hour whilst you get your posset on.

8. After half an hour roll out your pastry nice and thin (2mm) and using a pastry cutter cut the required size for your baking tray – I'm using a Yorkshire pud tray.

9. Place your pastry discs over each cup in the tray and gently press down until you have the pastry nice and straight.

10. You want the pastry shell to have perfect shape, so using rice or lentils, cover each pastry disc with a little cling film and add enough rice/lentils to hold the pastry in place so that it retains it's shape. If you don't do this the pastry may bubble and shrink.

11. Bake in the oven for around 6/7 mins, take the tray out and remove the cling film and grain and put back into the oven to brown all over. For roughly 3 to 4 mins. A darker pastry is infinitely better, but be careful not to overdo it, as it will become bitter.

12. Remove from the oven and cool in a dry place.

METHOD FOR POSSET

1. Place the double cream and sugar into a large pan and slowly bring to the boil. Then boil for 3 minutes.

2. Remove from the heat and allow to cool.

3. Add the sea-buckthorn or other citrus and whisk.

4. Pour into a container and refrigerate for at least 3 hours.

NOW TO PUT THE TARTS TOGETHER

1. Once your posset has set, using two tsps, spoon the posset into the tart shells, being careful not to over fill.

2. Cut the figs in half from the top down, then place each half on its flat side and cut into slices.

3. Add a slice of fig to each tart.

4. Dust with icing sugar.

AARON CRAZE

TV Chef

Chocolate Fondant-Soufflé

Chocolate fondant is a favourite with the ladies: the perfect choice for any fella who wants to impress his missis. Watch out though – when you've cooked it once you'll be making it all the time! It's particularly good served with vanilla ice cream.

~ INGREDIENTS ~

SERVES 6

- 3 tbsp cocoa powder, plus extra for dusting the moulds

- 100g good quality chocolate (70% cocoa solids) broken into small pieces

- 115g unsalted butter

- 3 free-range eggs, separated into yolks and whites

- 140g caster sugar

- Icing sugar for dusting

- Vanilla ice cream, to serve (optional)

⌒ METHOD ⌒

1. Place 6x125ml (4fl oz) ovenproof moulds or cups in a refrigerator to cool.

2. Preheat the oven to 200°C/400°F/Gas 6.

3. Put the cocoa, chocolate and 90g of the butter in a bowl sitting over a saucepan of simmering water. Make sure the bowl does not touch the water.

4. While the chocolate is melting, whisk the eggs yolks and sugar together in a bowl until runny. Have a clean bowl and a whisk ready to whisk the egg whites.

5. Stir the melted chocolate into the sweetened egg yolks. Set aside in a warm place.

6. Take the moulds out of the refrigerator. Melt the remaining butter and use a pastry brush to butter the insides of the moulds. Brush with straight strokes up the sides and over the rims.

Dust the buttered moulds with cocoa powder, tapping out any excess onto a sheet of baking paper.

7. Whisk the egg whites to stiff peaks. When stiff enough, you should be able to turn the bowl upside down without the froth falling out. Whisk a spoonful of the whites into the chocolate mixture, then very gently, fold in the rest.

8. Spoon the fluffy chocolate mixture into a large piping bag or a strong plastic sandwich bag with one corner cut off and fill the moulds. Scrape the tops level using the back of a knife, taking care not to rub off any butter from the rims.

9. Place the moulds on a baking sheet and bake until risen (about 10 minutes). Dust with icing sugar and serve immediately, with scoops of vanilla ice cream, if you like.

GLUTEN FREE/
HEALTHY OPTIONS

GARETH MALONE OBE

Choirmaster and presenter of the
TV series 'The Choir'

Orange Almond Cupcakes

I'd love to claim to be a baker of note but sadly the only cake I undertook would have made an excellent doorstop; this is why I delegate. Orange and citrus are my favourite flavours and this recipe is one for which I've been assistant baker to my wife Becky with responsibility for licking of spoons and washing up. The former I excelled at whilst the latter is still waiting for my attention...

INGREDIENTS

- 1 orange
- 2 eggs
- 6 tbsp agave nectar/runny honey
- 100g ground almonds
- 6 tbsp potato flour
- ½ tbsp baking powder

METHOD

1. Pre-heat the oven to 180°C/350°F/Gas 4.

2. Boil the orange for an hour then mash it up with a fork.

3. Whizz the orange in a blender, adding the rest of the ingredients one by one.

4. Spoon into 12 small cases and put in oven for 20–25 minutes depending on the heat of your oven. You might like to hover and check with a skewer for the last few minutes of cooking to avoid the cakes drying out.

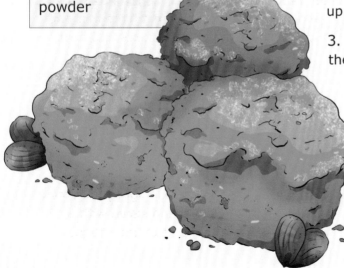

AINSLEY HARRIOTT
TV Chef/Author

Lemon Polenta Cake with Crème Fraiche

INGREDIENTS

- 250g softened butter
- 250g castor sugar
- 250g ground almonds
- 3 eggs
- 125g/4oz polenta
- Zest of 2 lemons
- Juice of 1 lemon
- ¾ tsp baking powder
- Crème Fraiche to serve

This is a wonderful cake to serve with afternoon tea, but works equally well as a dessert for a dinner party. It is practically gluten free (leave out the baking powder, or use a gluten free version for those with allergies) and it can be made with sunflower oil instead of butter (125 ml/8fl oz) for the perfect dairy free cake.

~ METHOD ~

1. Grease and base line a 9in/23cm loose-bottomed cake tin.

2. Set oven to 160°C/325°F/Gas 3.

3. Cream together butter and sugar into a bowl and incorporate the ground almonds. Add all the other ingredients and beat together until well mixed.

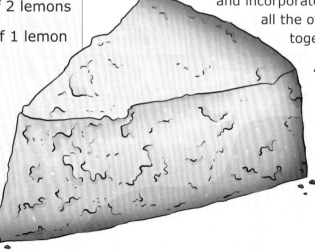

4. Pour into the prepared cake tin and bake in oven for 30–40 minutes until set in the middle and golden on the top.

5. Sprinkle lightly with icing sugar and serve with a dollop of crème fraiche.

JENNY ECLAIR

Comedienne

Wheat-free Clementine Cake

Here is the most delicious fruity, wheat free cake courtesy of Nigella Lawson, via my daughter, who is a bit gluten uneasy and tries to avoid dairy too – so ideal for those with lots of intolerances love Jenny xxx

~ METHOD ~

1. Put the clementines in a pot with cold water to cover, bring to the boil, and cook for 2 hours. Drain and, when cool, cut each clementine in half and remove the seeds. Then finely chop the skins, pith and fruit in the processor (or by hand, of course).

2. Preheat the oven to 190°C/375°F/Gas 5 Butter and line an 8-inch spring-form pan with parchment paper.

3. Beat the eggs by hand and then add the sugar, almonds, and baking powder.

4. Mix well, adding the chopped clementines. Alternatively, you can add all the other ingredients to the food processor and mix. Jenny doesn't like using the processor for this, and says,"you can't balk at a little light stirring!"

5. Pour the cake mixture into the prepared pan and bake for an hour, when a skewer will come out clean; you'll probably have to cover the cake with foil after about 40 minutes to stop the top from burning. Remove from the oven and leave to cool in the pan, on a rack. When the cake is cold, you can take it out of the pan. It is better a day after it's made, but you won't complain about eating it anytime.

INGREDIENTS

- 4–5 clementines (about 375g total weight)
- 6 eggs
- 225g sugar
- 250g ground almonds
- 1 heaped tsp baking powder

Clementine Cake recipe by Nigella Lawson taken from How to Eat, published by Chatto & Windus. Reprinted by permission of The Random House Group Limited

JO JOYNER

Actress

Gluten-free Banana Cake

~ METHOD ~

1. Pre-heat oven to 160°C/325°F/Gas 3.

2. Mix all the ingredients together. You can either mash the bananas for a consistently moist bread or I like to leave a few larger chopped bits as they make it interesting.

3. If you're adding pecans or fudge then add them last.

4. Line your loaf tin.

5. Bake for around 1 hour.

6. Remove and rest on a wire rack. If you think you have taken it out slightly early it should carry on cooking a little wrapped in tin foil.

7. Serve alone and warm with a cuppa!

8. Or yummy with good old-fashioned vanilla ice cream.

INGREDIENTS

- 170g Dove gluten free self-raising flour

- 170g caster sugar

- 170g butter

- 3 eggs

- 3 bananas (over ripe)

- Couple of drops of vanilla essence

- Optional - large handful of crushed pecan nuts or handful of broken up caramel fudge. As if it wasn't yummy enough the melted fudge is an extra treat. I tend to cut back a little on the sugar if I'm adding fudge.

THOMAS KELLER AND LENA KWAK

Chef/Author/Restaurateur
Research and Development Chef at the French Laundry in Yountville,
California/Founder with Thomas Keller of C4C, gluten-free flour.

Gluten-free Bouchons with Salted Caramel Frosting

◠INGREDIENTS◠

YIELD: 12 SERVINGS

FOR THE FROSTING :

- ⅓ cup granulated sugar

- 2 tbsp water

- ¼ cup heavy cream

- 1 tsp vanilla extract

- 1½ sticks butter, at room temperature

- 1 cup powdered sugar

- 1 tsp kosher salt

FOR THE BOUCHONS:

- 1½ sticks unsalted butter, melted and just slightly warm, plus more for the timbale molds

- ¾ cup gluten-free flour, preferably Cup4Cup, plus more for the timbale molds (See Cook's Note)

- 1 cup unsweetened cocoa powder

- 1 tsp kosher salt

- 3 large eggs

- 1½ cup plus 3 tablespoons granulated sugar

- ½ tsp vanilla extract

- 6 oz semisweet chocolate (such as 55% Valrhona Equatoriale), chopped into chocolate chip-size pieces

- Ice cream, for serving

~ METHOD ~

FOR THE FROSTING :

1. Place the sugar and water in a small saucepan over medium-high heat. Cook the sugar until it resembles caramel, turning thick in consistency and dark amber in color.

2. Remove from heat and whisk in the cream and vanilla extract. (Be sure to protect your arms as hot sugar tends to "jump" from the pan.) Set aside to cool completely.

3. In a mixer fitted with the paddle attachment, whip the butter until light and fluffy. Add the powdered sugar and salt, mixing until fully incorporated. Over medium speed, add the cooled caramel and beat until airy. Set aside.

FOR THE BOUCHONS:

1. Preheat the oven to 350 degrees.

2. Grease 12 timbale molds with butter and dust them with flour. Set aside.

3. Sift the flour, cocoa powder and salt into a bowl and set aside. In the bowl of a mixer fitted with the paddle attachment, mix together the eggs and sugar on medium speed until thick and very pale in color, about 3–5 minutes. Add the vanilla extract.

4. Reduce speed to low and add about one third of the dry ingredients, then one third of the butter, and continue alternating with the remaining flour and butter. Add the chocolate and mix to combine. (The batter can be refrigerated for up to 1 day.)

5. Put the timbale molds on a baking sheet. Place the batter in a pastry bag without a tip, or with a large plain tip, and fill each mold about two-thirds full.

6. Place in the oven and bake for 20–25 minutes. When the tops look shiny and set (like a brownie), test 1 cake with a wooden skewer or toothpick: It should come out clean but not dry (there may be some melted chocolate from the chopped chocolate). Transfer the bouchons to a cooling rack.

7. After 4–5 minutes, invert the timbale molds and let the bouchons cool upside down in the molds; then lift off the molds. (The bouchons are best eaten the day they are baked.) Frost and serve with ice cream, if desired.

NOTES AND SUBSTITUTIONS:

1. (Cook's Note: Cup4Cup flour is a gluten-free flour developed by chef Lena Kwak with the support of Thomas Keller. It can be found at Williams-Sonoma. If it is not available to you, replace with equal amounts of regular all-purpose flour.)

Adapted from "Bouchon" by Thomas Keller (Artisan, 2004)

Photograph: Harley Moon Kemp

SADIE FROST

Actress

Healthy Apple and Almond Cake
gf,wf,sf

INGREDIENTS

SERVES 4

- 50g coconut oil or butter at room temperature

- 50g xylitol

- 50g organic soya flour

- 50g ground almonds

- ½ tsp baking powder

- 50g flaked almonds plus 1 tbsp for sprinkling on top

- 150g organic apples (cored weight) unpeeled and diced

- 2 medium eggs

～ METHOD ～

1. Preheat oven to 180°C/350°F/Gas 4. Grease a 10cm/4in cake tin. (I use a bigger tin and it's fine.)

2. Cream together the coconut oil and xylitol together until soft and smooth.

3. Stir in the flour, baking powder and ground almonds together until the mixture resembles breadcrumbs.

4. Mix in the flaked almonds (reserving 1 tbsp) and apples, and then stir in the eggs without beating them.

5. Spoon into the prepared cake tin and sprinkle the reserved flaked almonds on top. Bake for 25 mins or until the top is golden and set. Remove from the oven and cover with tin foil, then return to the oven for a further 20 mins, or until the cake is cooked.

gf=gluten free wf=wheat free sf=sugar free

FERN BRITTON AND PHIL VICKERY

TV Presenter
TV Chef/Author

Gluten-free Zingy Lemon Cup Cakes

INGREDIENTS

12 SMALL CAKES

**Preparation time:
10 minutes**

**Cooking time:
15–20 minutes**

- 175g caster sugar

- 2 medium eggs, at room temperature

- 175g gluten-free flour

- 1½ level tsp gluten-free baking powder

- ½ tsp xanthan gum

- Finely grated zest of 1 large lemon

- 125ml/4fl oz rapeseed oil

- 125ml/4fl oz full cream milk

METHOD

1. Pre-heat the oven to 190°C/375°C/Gas 5. Line a muffin tin with cup cake cases.

2. Place the caster sugar and eggs into a mixing bowl and whisk on high speed for 2–3 minutes.

3. Mix the oil and milk together and set aside.

4. In another bowl, mix the flour, baking powder, xanthan gum and lemon zest together.

5. Once the eggs are thick enough to leave a trail, add the flour mix, the oil mix and fold all in well. The mixture should be quite soft and wet.

6. Fill the paper cases to about 1cm from the top and bake for 15–20 minutes until well risen and golden.

7. Remove and cool on a rack. Dust with icing sugar.

TIPS: These Little Light Cakes Are Lovely Just Dusted With Icing Sugar, But You Could Use The Lemon Juice Mixed To A Thick Paste With Some Fondant Icing Sugar, To Make A Glaze.

FREEZER: Cool, Wrap Well And Freeze In An Airtight Container.

COPYRIGHT PHIL VICKERY - OCTOBER 2011

GLYNIS BARBER

Actress

Gluten Dairy-free Chocolate Marble Cake

So good and moist no one will know.

~ INGREDIENTS ~

- 90g gluten and dairy free chocolate, melted (try Green and Blacks dark chocolate)

- 225g dairy free margarine (non-hydrogenated of course! I like the organic ones)

- 225g unrefined caster sugar

- 4 large eggs (beaten)

- 225g gluten free flour mix

- 2 tsp xanthan gum (the secret ingredient in all gluten free baking)

- 2½ tsp gluten free baking powder

- 1 tsp vanilla extract

- 3 tbsp milk alternative (I like almond milk)

~ METHOD ~

1. Pre-heat oven to 180°C/350°F/Gas 4.

2. Cream together the margarine and sugar then add the eggs and beat together well.

3. Sift in the flour, xanthan gum and baking powder. Fold together until well mixed.

4. Divide mixture in half.

5. To one half add the vanilla extract and milk, mix well.

6. Into the other half stir the melted chocolate.

7. In a 23cm/9 in square baking tin, lined with greaseproof paper, place alternate spoonfuls of the two mixtures.

8. Swirl a knife through the mixture many times and from different directions, to achieve a marbled effect.

9. Bake for 30–35 minutes.

10. Allow cake to cool completely before removing from tin.

Photograph: Gallina

DEBRA STEPHENSON

Impressionist/Actress/Comedienne/Singer

Gluten-free Chocolate Almond Traybake

INGREDIENTS

- 115g unsweetened dark chocolate

- ¾ cup butter

- 2 cups unrefined sugar

- 3 eggs

- 1 tsp Madagascar Bourbon vanilla

- 1 cup ground almonds

- 1 cup chopped pecans or walnuts

~ METHOD ~

1. Heat the oven to 170°C/325°F/Gas 4.

2. Line a tin with parchment paper.

3. Melt chocolate and butter in a pan on the hob.

4. Add sugar, eggs and vanilla.

5. Fold in the ground almonds and pecans.

6. Pour the mixture into the lined tin and bake for about 30–40 minutes depending on how gooey you like it.

7. Serve hot with ice cream.

8. Yum!!!

EMMA FREUD OBE

TV Presenter

Astonishing Miracle
Wheat-free, Sugar-free, Dairy-free
Lemon Drizzle Cake

You won't believe this cake could possibly taste great-but it's GORGEOUS. Whatever your diet, you can eat it in vast quantities!

INGREDIENTS

- 125ml/4fl oz good olive oil

- 150ml/5fl oz agave syrup

- 2 eggs

- 300g ground almonds

- Juice and zest of one lemon

- 1 heaped tsp baking powder

- Pinch of sea salt

FOR SYRUP

- Juice and zest of one lemon

- 1 tbsp agave syrup

METHOD

1. Line the base of an 18cm/7in square cake tin with parchment or greaseproof paper.

2. Preheat oven to 170°C/325°F/Gas 3.

3. Mix the olive oil with the agave syrup.

4. Add both eggs and beat for a few minutes.

5. Add the ground almonds, lemon juice and zest, baking powder and salt and mix gently.

6. Pour the batter into prepared cake tin and bake for 30 minutes or until golden and your knife comes out clean.

7. Take out of oven and leave in tin and prick it gently all over with a toothpick.

8. Mix lemon juice and zest with a tablespoon of agave syrup in a pan over a low heat until warm.

9. Once combined, spoon the warm drizzle all over the top of the cake and leave to cool.

10. Remove from tin and remove paper.

11. Eat. Marvel. Enjoy!

SOPHIE MICHELL

Chef/Author/TV Presenter

Mum's Wheat-free Hazelnut Cake

My mother was an amazing cook and everyone having supper together each evening was very important to her. Cakes and sweet were not her strong point though, apart from this one! It's now one of my favourites, I love the nutty, moist chewiness of it and I don't eat wheat, so that's a huge bonus. It's doesn't taste like a healthy cake though and I top it off with chocolate sauce and whipped cream for a super indulgent dessert

INGREDIENTS

SERVES 12

PREP TIME 10 MINUTES

COOKING TIME 35–40 MINUTES

- 300g whole hazelnuts
- 300g caster sugar
- 8 egg whites

METHOD

1. Preheat the oven to 180°C/375°F/Gas 5. Lightly oil a deep 20cm/8in, spring-form cake tin and the line the base with a circle of parchment or baking paper.

2. Blitz the hazelnuts and sugar in a blender together until fine. Separate the eggs and add the whites to a large clean mixing bowl, keep the egg yolks for another recipe.

3. Whisk the whites to soft peaks, then gently fold in the nut mixture. Pour the mixture into the tin and then bake for 35–40 minutes until risen and golden brown.

4. Serve with some crème fraiche and if feeling very naughty, some chocolate sauce.

CATHERINE TYLDESLEY

Actress

Chocolate and Orange Cake

INGREDIENTS

- 150g dark chocolate (I like Green & Blacks best)

- 100g unsalted butter (and a little extra for greasing)

- 6 large free-range eggs

- 150g ground almonds

- Grated zest of 2 oranges

- 2 tbsp freshly squeezed orange juice

- 100g caster sugar

- 3 tbsp cocoa

~ METHOD ~

1. Preheat the oven to 170°C/325°F/Gas 3. Grease a 23cm/9in deep cake tin with butter and line the base with baking paper (don't forget this bit! I always do and it gets messy!)

2. Break the chocolate into squares and put in a bowl with the butter. Place the bowl over a pan of simmering water until the chocolate has melted – don't let the base touch the water! Leave to cool slightly.

3. Separate the egg yolks from the whites. Stir the ground almonds, orange zest, juice and yolks into the chocolate (I usually start drooling at this point). In a different bowl whisk the egg whites until stiff, add the sugar 1 tbsp at a time - after each spoonful whisk again until stiff. Add a quarter to the chocolate mixture and gently fold in. Then fold in the rest of the egg whites.

4. Turn the mixture into the cake tin and bake for 35-40 minutes. Leave to cool for ten minutes. Then turn out and finish cooling on a wire rack. Finish with a dusting of cocoa. I think this is best served with a large scoop of vanilla ice-cream...but then I am greedy! ENJOY!

ADAM SIMMONDS

Head Chef at Danesfield House

Diabetic and Gluten-free Chocolate Chip Cookies

INGREDIENTS

MAKES: APPROX 12 COOKIES

- 85g unsalted butter

- 28g Splenda Sweetener (available from health food shops)

- ½ tsp vanilla essence

- ¼ tsp salt

- 165g gluten-free flour

- 1 small free-range egg

- 38g dark chocolate chips

~ METHOD ~

1. Pre-heat the oven to 190°C/375°F/Gas 5.

2. Beat together the butter and Splenda.

3. Add the salt and gluten free flour and mix well.

4. Add the eggs and mix to form a dough.

5. Finally add the chocolate chips and mix together.

6. Split the cookie dough into 30g/1 oz pieces and roll between the palms of your hands to form balls roughly the size of apricots.

7. Place these on a baking tray lined with greaseproof paper and flatten each one gently with the palm of your hand, making sure you leave space between each one, as they will spread slightly.

8. Bake for 10–15 minutes or until the cookies start to brown around the edges.

9. Remove from the tray and place onto a wire cooling rack and allow to cool.

RACHEL STEVENS

Singer/Actress/Finalist on
Strictly Come Dancing 2008

Gluten-free Citrus Polenta Cake

~ INGREDIENTS ~

- 140g ground almonds

- 100g polenta

- 1 tsp gluten-free baking powder

- 4 large organic eggs separated

- 170ml/5¾ fl oz grapeseed oil

- 170g caster sugar

- Grated zest of 1 orange

- Grated zest of 1 lemon

SYRUP

- 150ml/5fl oz orange juice

- 55g caster sugar

MASCARPONE CREAM

- 250g mascarpone

- 40g icing sugar sifted

- 220ml/8fl oz double cream whipped to soft peaks

~ METHOD ~

1. Preheat the oven to 180°C/160°C Fan/ Gas 4 and lightly grease a cake tin about 20x7.5cm (8x3in). Mix together the ground almonds, polenta and baking powder.

2. In a separate bowl, beat the egg yolks, grapeseed oil, 150g/5oz of the caster sugar, and the orange and lemon zests, until smooth. Add the dry ingredients to the egg mixture, folding gently.

3. Whisk the egg whites and the remaining caster sugar in a clean bowl until stiff peaks form and add these to the cake mixture in three additions.

4. Pour into the prepared tin and bake in the centre of the preheated oven for 30–35 minutes or until a skewer inserted at the centre of the cake comes out clean. Leave the cake to cool in the tin while you make the syrup.

5. Place the orange juice and caster sugar in a small saucepan over a low heat. Stir to dissolve the sugar, bring to the boil and boil for 1 minute. Leave to cool for 10 minutes.

6. Pierce the cake all over through to the bottom with a skewer, then drizzle the warm syrup over the cake. Leave for 10 minutes before turning out of the tin and leave to cool completely.

7. Meanwhile, make the mascarpone cream: combine the mascarpone and sifted icing sugar in a small bowl, then fold in the whipped cream.

8. Serve the cake with the mascarpone cream (or alternatively you can use the cream to frost the top of the cake).

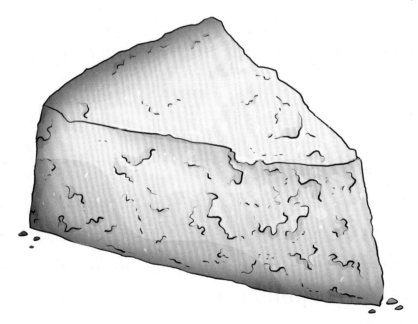

Taken from the Clean & Lean Cookbook courtesy of the Cupcake Company

Make-up artist

Flapjacks

-~ METHOD ~-

1. Pre-heat oven to 190°C /375°F/Gas 5.

2. Lightly grease a shallow tin measuring approximately 30x18.5cm or 13x7½ in.

3. Melt the butter in a medium saucepan, and add the vanilla extract.

4. Weigh out the xylitol, then weigh the agave nectar by spooning it on top of the xylitol.

5. Add this to the melted butter and heat through.

6. Remove the pan from the heat and add the oats, and dried fruit, seeds, and fold together well.

7. Spread the mixture in the tin and pat down to make sure it is even. Bake for 20–25 minutes until just golden brown.

8. Be careful not to over bake it as it will make the flapjacks too hard and crunchy.

9. As soon as you take them out of the oven score them into bars and leave in the tin to cool.

10. While the flapjack is cooling, melt the chocolate (very gently) over simmering water or in the microwave.

11. Dip each flapjack in the melted chocolate and chill in the fridge before serving.

INGREDIENTS
-~•~-

- 170g organic butter, unsalted

- 110g xylitol

- 55g agave nectar

- 225g organic gluten free oats

- 100g dried mixed organic fruit and seeds, roughly chopped (apricots, dates, raisins, pumpkin seeds etc.)

- 1 tsp vanilla extract

- 100g organic dark chocolate

Photograph Steve Lee

JUN TANAKA

Food Network Chef and
Co-founder of Street Kitchen

Gluten-free Chocolate Pudding

INGREDIENTS

SERVES 8

- 375g dark chocolate 70%

- 300g sugar

- 300g unsalted butter

- 9 eggs

~ METHOD ~

1. Place the chocolate and butter in a metal bowl and place on top of a pan of simmering water until melted.

2. Mix the eggs and sugar in a bowl (don't whisk too much).

3. Fold the melted chocolate into the eggs and sugar.

4. Lightly butter and sugar the pudding bowls and spoon in the mixture until it is 2cm from the top.

5. Bake in the oven at 180ºC/350ºF/Gas 4 for 10 minutes.

6. Serve with a scoop of vanilla ice cream.

~ BEN KINSELLA TRUST ~

Ben Kinsella

In June 2008, our family was devastated when our beautiful Ben went out one night and never came home again. We lost Ben to the growing problem of knife crime – an issue that you may think will never affect you or your loved ones, but which Ben's story proves may sadly not be the case. Ben was quite simply in the wrong place at the wrong time and for no reason whatsoever his life was taken, while the lives of his family and friends will never be the same again.

Ben was a sixteen-year-old boy who loved life. He loved his family and friends, his dog Teddy, football, art, music and girls! He had a heart of gold and was the biggest clown there ever was, always trying to make people laugh in any way he could. His ambition was to be a graphic designer and for his GCSE exams, he produced some amazing work but never got to learn of the A* grades he received for it. Anybody who knew Ben knew what a special, caring and fun-loving boy he was – he is very deeply missed.

Another passion of Ben's was cooking. He loved spending hours in the kitchen creating exotic and messy recipes using every saucepan in the house - which Mum would then have to wash up after. It is therefore very fitting to have a cookbook produced in his memory and we know he would have loved cooking and tasting every single recipe in this book!

Ben's favourite dessert was Apple Pie and you will find his recipe in here. If you do make this recipe, please remember Ben fondly while

BEN KINSELLA TRUST

doing so - he would be so happy to know that in some small way he is still producing a mess in the kitchen ;o)

After losing Ben, we set up a Trust in his name to keep his memory alive and to try and create some positivity from his short but incredible life. As a Trust we aim to:

● Pass on the legacy of Ben

● Promote knife-crime awareness

● Educate children of all ages to be aware of the consequences of knife crime and what it can do to a family.

To do this we have built an interactive exhibition which will go into schools and communities around the country in the near future. It is very emotional and thought-provoking and will hopefully have an impact and help reduce knife crime in this country.

We would like to pass on our gratitude to all who have made this book possible – to Linda Morris and her team, to everyone who contributed a recipe, to the Food Network Channel UK for their sponsorship and of course to the publishers for all their hard work.
We would also like to thank you for buying this book as in doing so a donation has been made to The Ben Kinsella Trust and without the generosity of your donations, we would not be able to do the work we do.

The Kinsella Family & Ben

www.benkinsella.org.uk

243

FOOD NETWORK

Whet your appetite with...

Mouth-watering baking shows:

- The frosting guns are out in *Cupcake Wars*, the tastiest competition yet
- *DC Cupcakes* offers sweet success for two sisters in the baking business
- Dream about desserts in *Unique Sweets*
- *Ace of Cakes*, cake creations with attitude

British Faces and Flavours:

Food Network UK chef Andy Bates 'aka the Pie Man' offers a twist on British classics in *Street Feasts*. Make his melt-in-the-mouth tarts and tune in for his new series touring America.

Don't forget to check out Reza Mahammad's unforgettable tour of India's regal residences. Next stop Africa in *Reza's African Kitchen*.

Popular favourites:

- *Diners, Drive-ins and Dives*, hosted by 'rock star chef' Guy Fieri
- Adam Richman's trailblazing *Man v. Food Nation*

The Icing on the Cake:

- Ina Garten's *Barefoot Contessa*: enjoy her incredibly elegant and easy recipes
- Guy Fieri in *Guy's Big Bite*: a show about fearless, fun food

Watch our programming online
www.foodnetwork.co.uk

INDEX

INDEX

INDEX

~ INDEX ~

BAKING BELLES

"The Baking Belles" who set out to compile this book comprises the following people:

(from left to right, Lindsay Shaerf, Elisa Margolin, Linda Morris, Ingrid Salida, Anouska Plaut)

Linda Morris – enjoys baking and is mother to a professional chef, Ed Shaerf (Chef Patron at One Blenheim Terrace).

Ingrid Salida – loves cooking and volunteered to be our Home Economist.

Lindsay Shaerf – is our legal eagle, a solicitor and wife to Ed Shaerf and bakes delicious cakes.

Anouska Plaut – is a childbirth educator, journalist, great cake baker and mother to two young children.

Elisa Margolin – is a fantastic novelty cake baker and mother to two young children.